NELSON BLACKIE

MATHS
IN ACTION
PLUS

AUTHORS

G. Brown   St Anne's RC High School, Stockport
G. Marra   Linlathen High School, Dundee
K. Methven   Jedburgh Grammar School
E. Mullan   Galashiels Academy
R. Murray   Hawick High School
J. Thomson   Galashiels Academy

STUDENTS' BOOK

Thomas Nelson and Sons Ltd
Nelson House Mayfield Road
Walton-on-Thames Surrey
KT12 5PL UK

Nelson Blackie
Wester Cleddens Road
Bishopbriggs
Glasgow
G64 2NZ UK

Thomas Nelson Australia
102 Dodds Street
South Melbourne
Victoria 3205 Australia

Nelson Canada
1120 Birchmount Road
Scarborough Ontario
MIK 5G4 Canada

Cover photograph by David Usill

© G. Brown, G. Marra, K. Methven, E. Mullan, R. Murray and J. Thomson 1995

First published by Thomas Nelson and Sons Ltd 1995
IⓉP Thomas Nelson is an International Thomson Publishing Company
IⓉP is used under licence

ISBN 0-17-431446-9
NPN 9 8 7 6 5 4 3 2 1

Printed in Great Britain by Hobbs the Printers Ltd,
Totton, Hampshire SO40 3YS

CONTENTS

1 WHOLE NUMBERS IN ACTION

Order

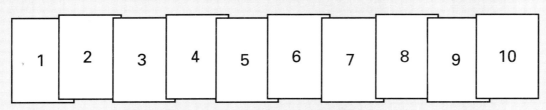

These ten cards are in order.

If you mix them up and remove one,
it is hard to spot which card is missing.

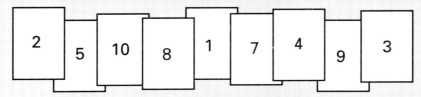

Which card *is* missing?
Put the cards in order: 1, 2, 3, ... until you find out.

EXERCISE 1

1 Find the missing card in each case:

a

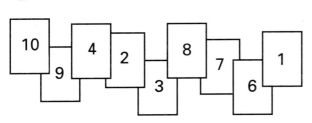

b

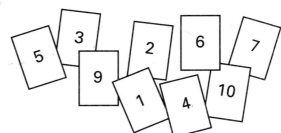

2 Which card is turned over?

a

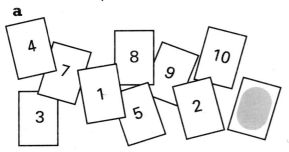

b

3 Mike bought ten raffle tickets, numbered 51 to 60.

When he won he gave up the winning ticket.

What was the winning ticket?

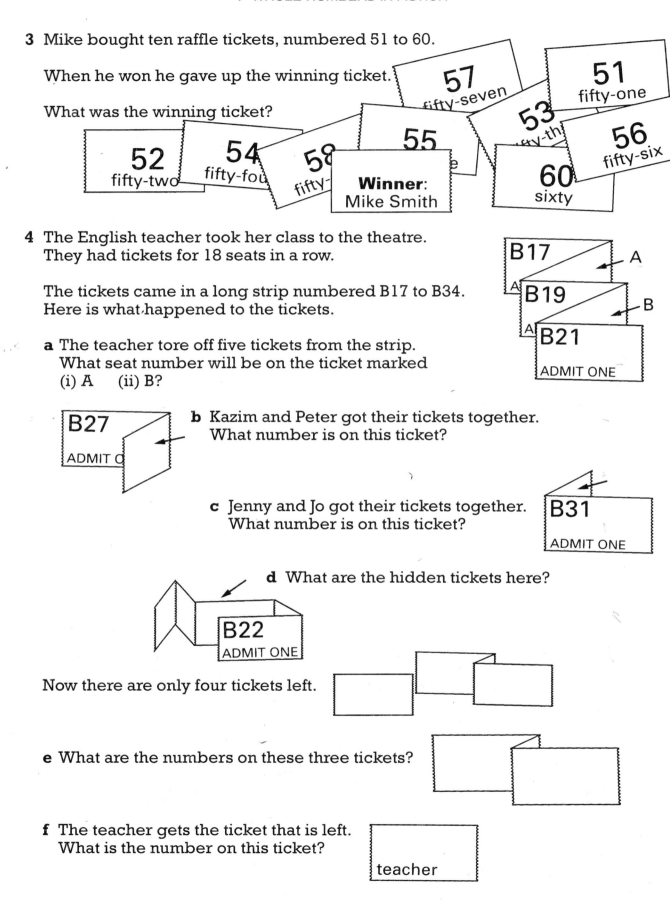

57 fifty-seven

51 fifty-one

53 fifty-th

55

56 fifty-six

52 fifty-two

54 fifty-fou

58 fifty-

Winner: Mike Smith

60 sixty

4 The English teacher took her class to the theatre.
They had tickets for 18 seats in a row.

The tickets came in a long strip numbered B17 to B34.
Here is what happened to the tickets.

B17 A

A B19 B

A B21

ADMIT ONE

a The teacher tore off five tickets from the strip.
What seat number will be on the ticket marked
(i) A   (ii) B?

B27

ADMIT O

b Kazim and Peter got their tickets together.
What number is on this ticket?

c Jenny and Jo got their tickets together.
What number is on this ticket?

B31

ADMIT ONE

d What are the hidden tickets here?

B22

ADMIT ONE

Now there are only four tickets left.

e What are the numbers on these three tickets?

f The teacher gets the ticket that is left.
What is the number on this ticket?

teacher

2

Twenty-one

Mark and Sara play a card game.
They add up their cards.
The person closer to 21 wins.

Mark scores
6 + 10 = 16

Sara scores
9 + 8 = 17

Sara wins!

EXERCISE 2

1 Who wins here?

a

b

2 In the game you are allowed to take another card.
Your score must *not* go over 21 or you lose.
Who wins?

a

b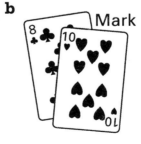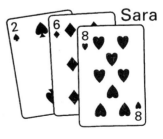

c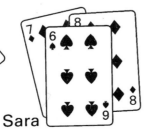

d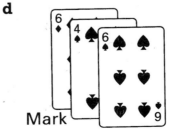

3 What must the hidden card be to make each add up to 21?

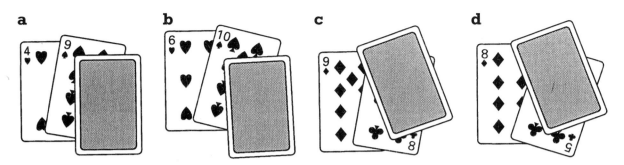

a   **b**   **c**   **d**

4 What is the smallest the hidden card can be if:

a John is to beat Mark?

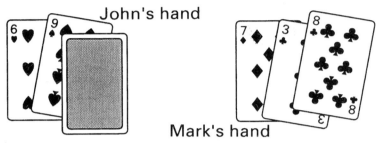

John's hand

Mark's hand

b Ben is to beat Moira?

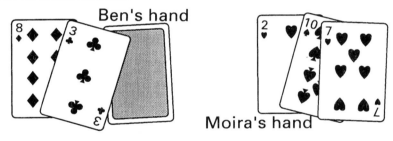

Ben's hand

Moira's hand

5 A 'five card trick' is when you have five cards which add up to 21 or less.

Example   Total = 20 ... a five card trick.

Which of these are five card tricks?

a   **b**   **c**   **d**

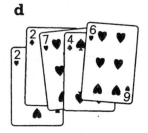

Racing Cards

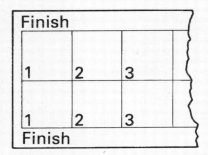

Finish			
1	2	3	
1	2	3	
Finish			

			Start
17	18	19	20
17	18	19	20
			Start

Racing Cards

Farah is playing a board game with Michael.
Each has a horse running in a lane.
Farah has the black horse and Michael has the white.
They both start on square 20.
Farah picks up a 5 of diamonds.
She moves to square 15 because 20 − 5 = 15.

15	16

EXERCISE 3

1 Michael is on 20. He turns over a 7.

$$20 - 7 = \boxed{}$$

What square does he land on?

2 Farah is on 15. She turns over a 6.

$$15 - 6 = \boxed{}$$

What square does she land on?

3 It is Michael's turn again.
From question **1** you know he is on square 13.
He turns over an 8.

$$13 - 8 = \boxed{}$$

What square does he land on?

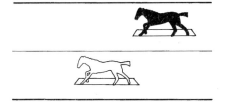

4 What card must Farah turn over to reach square 1 and the finish?

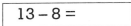

5 During different games:

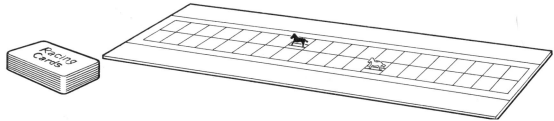

a Lorna moved from square 12 to square 2.
What is the number on the card she turned over?

b Jack moved from square 18 to square 9.
What is the number on the card he turned over?

c Dean moved from square 17 to square 9.
What is the number on the card he turned over?

6 Ben starts at square 20.

He turns over a 4, then a 7 and then a 5.

a Which square does he land on after:
(i)   turning over the 4
(ii) *then* turning over the 7
(iii) *then* the 5?

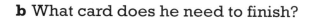

b What card does he need to finish?

7 Jane started on square 20, then landed on square 17,
then on square 12, and then on square 5.

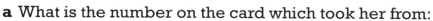

a What is the number on the card which took her from:
(i)   square 20 to square 17
(ii) square 17 to square 12
(iii) square 12 to square 5?

b What card does she need to finish?

8  Jane's brother, Austin, turned over two cards.
These let him move from square 17 to square 9.
What might have been the numbers on the two cards?

Darts

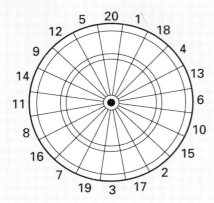

Darts is a game played on a board like this.

A dart right in the middle scores 50.

A dart in the small area around the middle scores 25.

EXERCISE 4

1 What does each person score here?

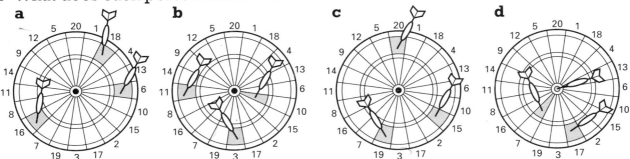

   a   **b**   **c**   **d**

2 Sometimes a dart misses. It then scores nothing.
What does each person score here?

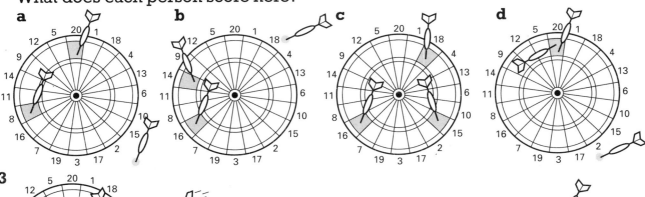

   a   **b**   **c**   **d**

3

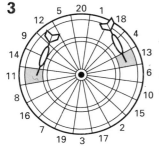

Khalid wants to score a total of 36.
Two darts are already thrown.
Where should he aim his third dart?

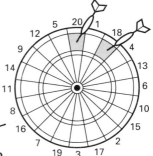

    4 Tina wants to score a total of 57.
Two darts are already thrown.
Where should she aim her third dart?

5 A dart in the middle thin ring scores three times the usual amount.

A dart in the outer thin ring scores two times the usual amount.

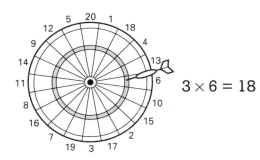

$3 \times 6 = 18$

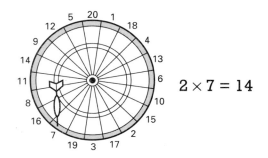

$2 \times 7 = 14$

What do these darts score?

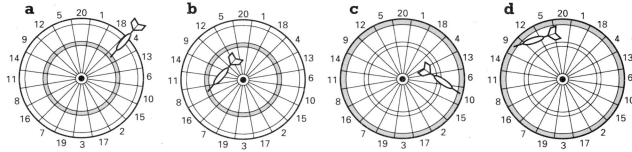

a   **b**   **c**   **d**

A dart in the middle thin ring scores **treble** $3 \times 4 = 12$
A dart in the outer thin ring scores **double** $2 \times 10 = 20$
A dart anywhere else scores **single** 17
So the player here scores $12 + 20 + 17 = 49$.

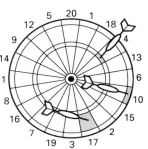

6 Work out these scores.

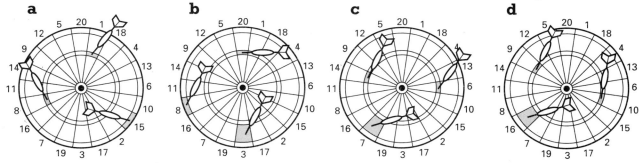

a   **b**   **c**   **d**

7 Work out the total score for each of the following:

a

John	single 14
	double 12
	double 5

b

Paul	single 18
	double 19
	treble 20

c

Gemma	double 17
	double 4
	treble 12

d

Richard	treble 5
	double 13
	treble 6

Fortune's Wheel

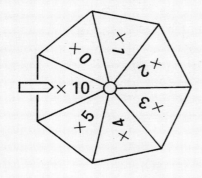

Adam	Bibi	Cath	Doug
5	5	5	5

Each player starts with 5 points.
The wheel is spun. The scores are multiplied.

Adam spun. He got

His score is now 20.

5 — × 4 — 20

EXERCISE 5

1 a Bibi spins next.

She gets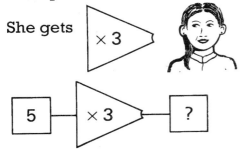

5 — × 3 — ?

What is Bibi's score now?

c Doug's spin stops at

5 — × 0 — ?

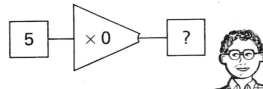

Work out Doug's score.

b Now it is Cath's turn.

The wheel stops at

5 — × 5 — ?

What is Cath's score now?

d Check that their scores are right.

Adam	Bibi	Cath	Doug
20	15	25	0

2 a In round 2 Adam spins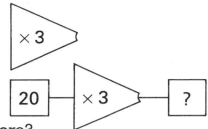

What is Adam's new score?

b Bibi gets $\times 5$. Cath spins $\times 2$. Doug turns up $\times 5$.

What does the scoreboard look like now?

Adam	Bibi	Cath	Doug
60	?	?	?

3 In round 3 the spins were as follows:

Adam	$\times 2$
Bibi	$\times 1$
Cath	$\times 3$
Doug	$\times 4$

Work out the scores after round 3.

4 In round 4 Doug spun $\times 10$ but it made no difference. He still had nothing.

The picture shows the results after round 4.

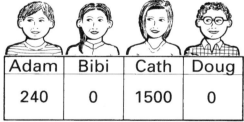

Adam	Bibi	Cath	Doug
240	0	1500	0

What did each player spin on Fortune's Wheel in round 4?

5 In a different part of the game each player starts with 1.
Find each player's final score if the spins were:

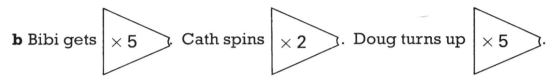

Adam	$\times 2$;	$\times 3$;	$\times 1$;	$\times 10$
Bibi	$\times 5$;	$\times 4$;	$\times 0$;	$\times 3$
Cath	$\times 2$;	$\times 3$;	$\times 4$;	$\times 1$
Doug	$\times 3$;	$\times 5$;	$\times 10$;	$\times 2$

A	B	C	D
?	?	?	?

Sharing Out

A set of dominoes contains 28 tiles.

To start a game the tiles are shared out equally. Any left over are kept in a separate pile.

If three people are playing they each get ...

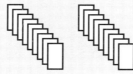

... 9 tiles and there will be 1 left over.

$28 \div 3 = 9$ remainder 1

EXERCISE 6

---

1 a $28 \div 4 = ?$ remainder?   Describe how you would share out the dominoes among four players.

b $28 \div 5 = ?$ remainder?   Describe how you would share out the dominoes among five players.

c $28 \div 6 = ?$ remainder?   Describe how you would share out the dominoes among six players.

d How many dominoes would each player get if there were ten players?

2 A bigger set of dominoes contains 55 tiles.

Describe how they would be shared out equally among:
a 3 players   **b** 4 players
c 5 players   **d** 10 players.

3 There are 52 cards in a pack.

Describe how they would be dealt out equally among:

a 3 players   **b** 4 players
c 5 players   **d** 10 players.

4

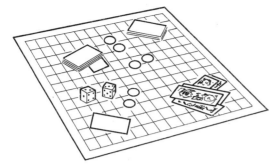

At the start of a board game £720 is shared out among the players.

How much does each get if there are:

a 3 players
b 4 players
c 5 players
d 10 players?

5 When he was playing the board game, Jim turned over this card.

There are four other players.

What does each get if Jim has:
a £20   **b** £80   **c** £48?

Bad luck!

Share your money out among the other players.

6

Good news
You've won £600.
Bad news
Give it to the other players.

During another game Jim picked this card.

How should the money be divided if there are:

a 3 others   **b** 4 others
c 5 others   **d** 10 others?

7 During a game with five players Jim lands on this square.

Bonanza!

Share out the bank.

How much does each player get if the bank has:

a   £600
b   £1000
c   £960?

CHECK-UP ON WHOLE NUMBERS

1 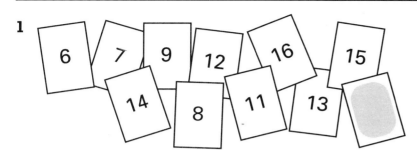 Put the cards in order to help you decide what the mystery card is.

2 a What is the total of each hand?

   b Who has the higher total?

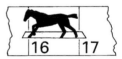

Alice   Becky

3

Tom   Lawrence

  a Tom has a total of 19.
What is his hidden card worth?

  b Lawrence has a total of 22.
What is the value of his hidden card?

4 a $18 - 7 = ?$ **b** $17 - 9 = ?$

  c Calum is playing the Horse Racing Game.

    He is on square 16.

    He turns over a 9.

    | $16 - 9 =$ |

    On which square does he land?

5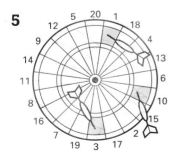

  a What did Ryan score?

  b What did Claire score?
(Remember the doubles and trebles.)

Ryan   Claire

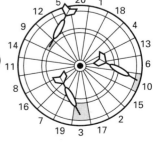

6

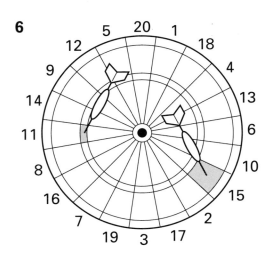

Rajiv needs 53 points.

a How many points does he have so far?

b Where should he aim the last dart to get a total of 53?

7 Work out each of the following:

a 17×4 **b** 25×3 **c** 74×5 **d** 35×10

e $40 \div 4$ **f** $35 \div 5$ **g** $42 \div 3$ **h** $500 \div 10$

8 Ten coins are shared equally among four people. Some coins are left.

a How many coins does each person get?
b How many coins are left?

9

Master Bun
The
Baker's Son

Happy Families is a card game which uses a pack of 60 cards.

They are shared out equally.

How many cards does each player get if there are:

a 4 players   **b** 5 players
c 6 players   **d** 10 players?

Corners

Take a piece of scrap paper.

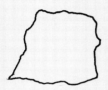

Fold it in half.

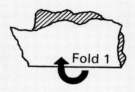

Fold it in half again along fold 1.

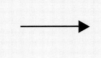

Check that the corner you have formed fits the corner of your book.

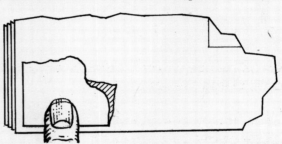

This shape you have made is called a **right angle**.

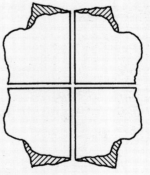

Make four of these corners in the same way. If you have made them correctly, then all four will fit together as shown.

You can use the template you made to look for right angles.

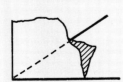

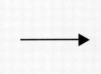

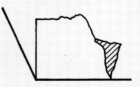

It is too big to fit in this corner.

It fits this corner perfectly. This corner is a **right angle**.

It is too small to fit this corner.

EXERCISE 1

1 Use your template to find the right angles in this collection.

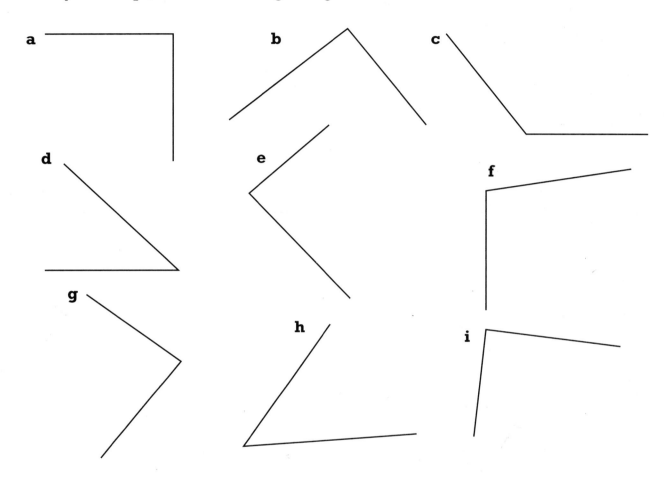

2 Rory has a room with five corners. Here is a plan of the room.
Use your template to find the right angles.

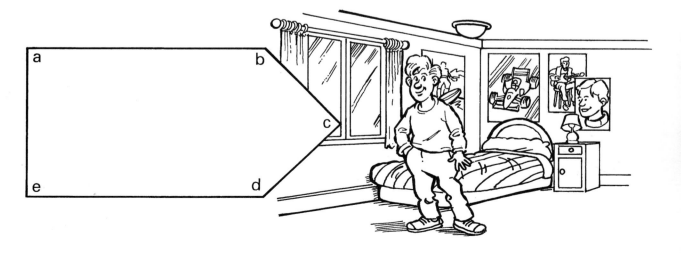

Marking Right Angles

When we draw a **right angle**
we mark the corner with a box.

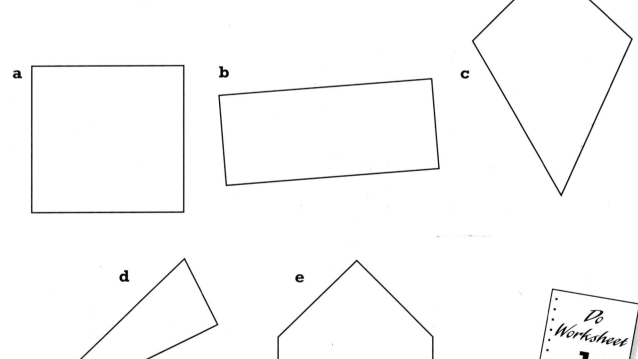

EXERCISE 2

Trace the following shapes.

Use your template to spot the right angles.

Mark each right angle on your tracing with a box.

a

b

c

d

e

Do
Worksheet
1

Smaller or Larger?

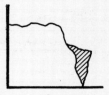

This angle is **smaller** than a right angle.

This angle is a right angle.

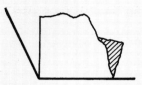

This angle is **larger** than a right angle.

EXERCISE 3

Use your template to help you complete Worksheet 2 for the angles below.

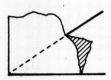

Get Worksheet **2**

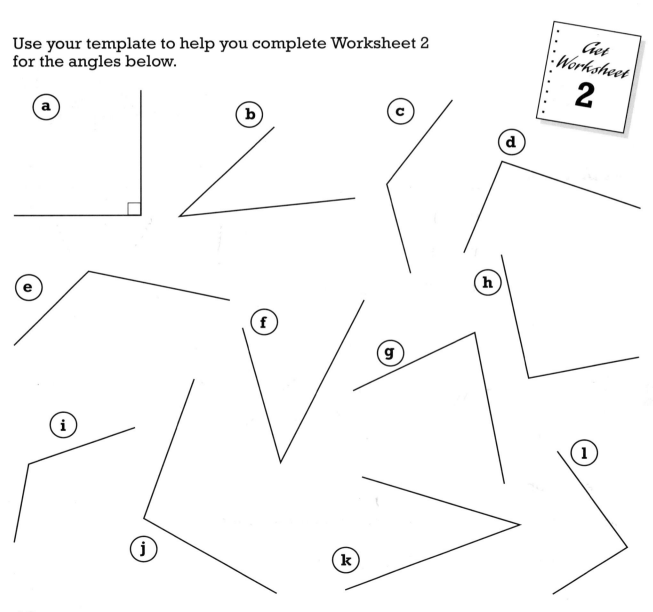

Measuring

Length is measured in **centimetres**. This line is 4 cm long.

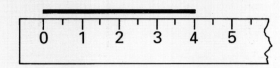

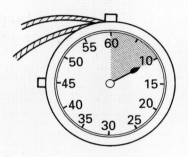

Time is measured in **seconds**.

The hand shows that 10 seconds have passed.

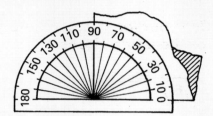

Angles are measured in **degrees**.

A right angle has 90 degrees. We write this as 90°.

EXERCISE 4

1 Place two templates together.

Two right angles make a straight line.

How many degrees make a straight line?

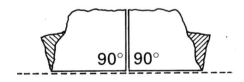

2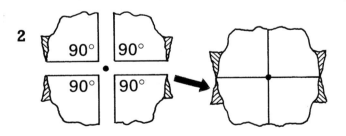

Place four templates together.

Four right angles fit round a point.

How many degrees fit round a point?

3 Open up one of your templates.

Mark a point where you see four right angles meeting.

How many degrees are round this point?

Open and Closed

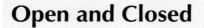

The comic is closed.
This angle is 90°.

The comic is open.
This angle is 180°.

EXERCISE 5

1 Sue buys a pop poster.

Here is a picture of it closed ...

a How many degrees?

... half open ...

b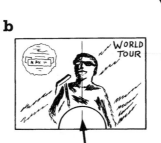

c 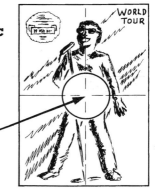 How many degrees?

... and fully opened.

2 Bruce is folding his map away.

a Open 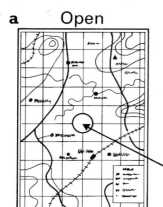 What size of angle is this?

b Half closed  What size of angle is this?

c Closed  What size of angle is this?

Types of Angles

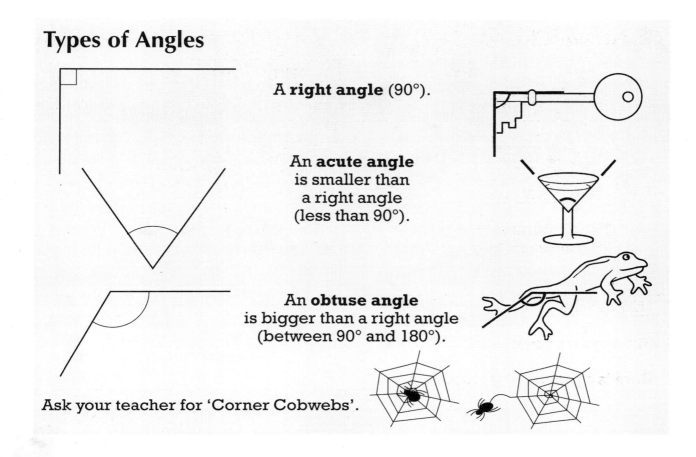

A **right angle** (90°).

An **acute angle** is smaller than a right angle (less than 90°).

An **obtuse angle** is bigger than a right angle (between 90° and 180°).

Ask your teacher for 'Corner Cobwebs'.

EXERCISE 6

1 Say whether the angles below are **right**, **acute** or **obtuse**.

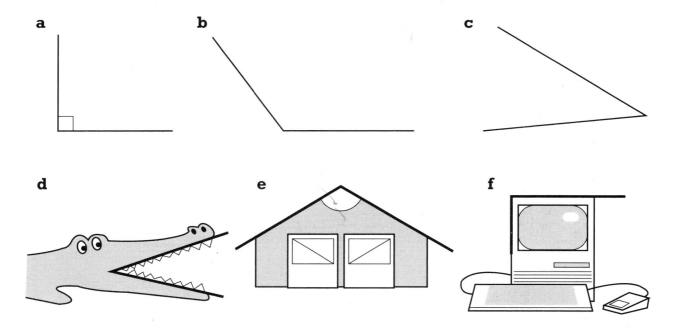

a

b

c

d

e

f

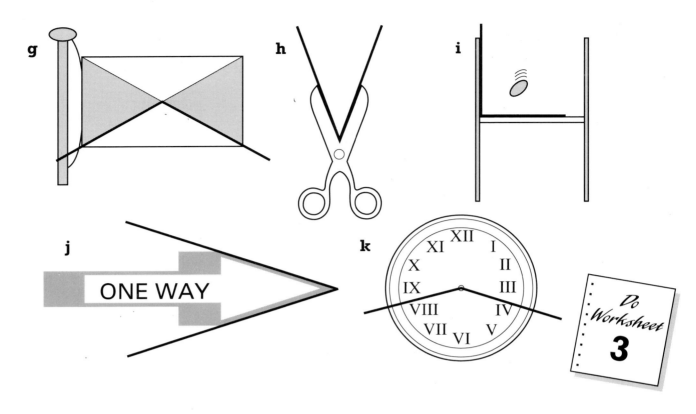

g

h

i

j

ONE WAY

k

Do Worksheet **3**

2 There are eight right angles to be found in this gate. Try to find them all.

3

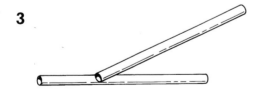

Two straws can be placed so that they form an acute angle and an obtuse angle at the same time.

Show how two straws can be placed so that they form:
a two right angles
b a straight line
c four right angles
d two acute angles and two obtuse angles.

Ask your teacher for 'Tarantula Towers'.

CHECK-UP ON ANGLES

1 Use a template to pick out the right angles on the side of this house.

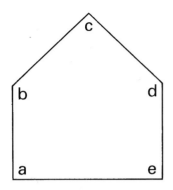

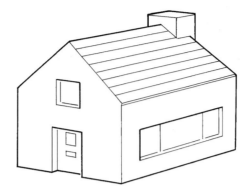

2 a How many degrees make a right angle?

b How many degrees make a straight line?

c How many degrees fit round a point?

3 Say whether each angle is acute, obtuse, right or straight.

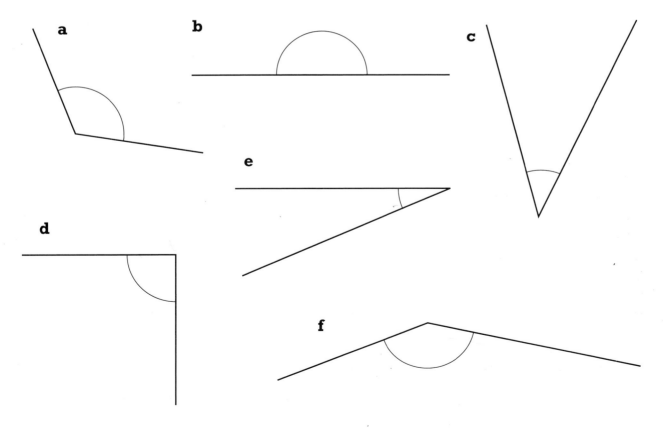

LETTERS AND NUMBERS

Missing Numbers

In the science lab the drawers are labelled.

Some labels are missing.

We can still work out what they are by looking at the pattern of numbers around them.

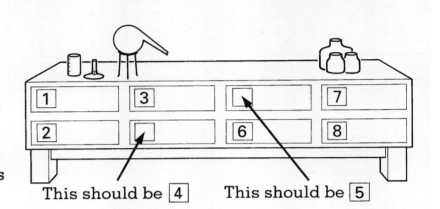

This should be 4   This should be 5

EXERCISE 1

1 In each street some of the house numbers have fallen off.

Help the postman work out the missing numbers.

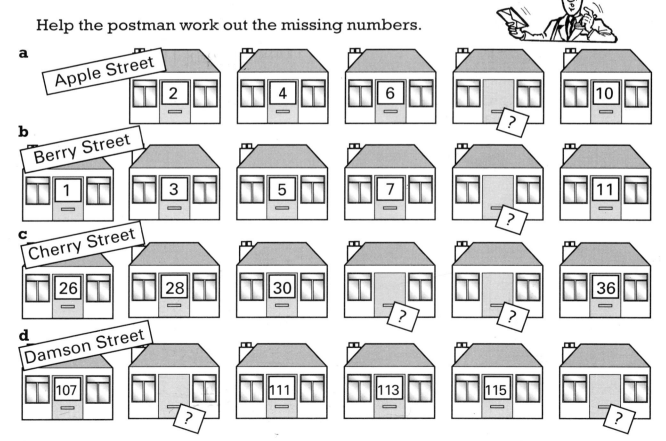

a   Apple Street   2   4   6   ?   10

b   Berry Street   1   3   5   7   ?   11

c   Cherry Street   26   28   30   ?   ?   36

d   Damson Street   107   ?   111   113   115   ?

2 Jan was laying out cards in patterns.
Guess the cards which are turned over.

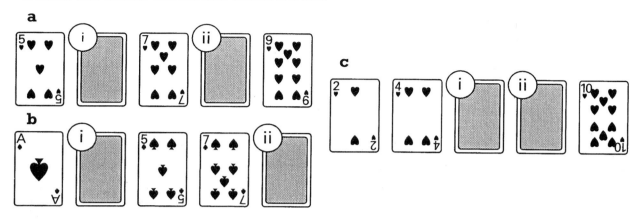

3 The lift can only carry 11 people.

a Four people are in the lift.
How many more can get in?

$$4 + \boxed{} = 11$$

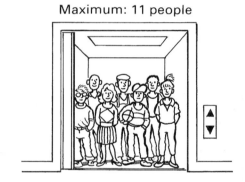

b How many more can get in?

$$7 + \boxed{} = 11$$

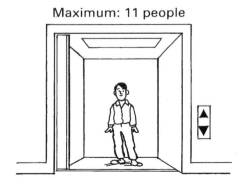

c How many more can get in?

$$1 + \boxed{} = 11$$

d Oops! 13 people in the lift.
How many have to get out?

$$13 - \boxed{} = 11$$

4 What number goes in each box?

a 3 + ☐ = 7   **b** 8 + 5 = ☐   **c** ☐ + 7 = 12

d 9 − ☐ = 3   **e** ☐ − 2 = 7   **f** 14 − ☐ = 6

5

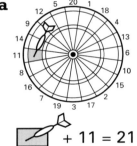

Score 21 with two darts and win a prize!

How much more is needed to win in each case?

a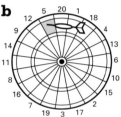

☐ + 11 = 21

b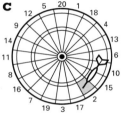

5 + ☐ = 21

c

21 − 2 = ☐

6 Belinda is making up puzzles with cards.

5 + X = 9

Barry says 'x = 4' because must be 4

Solve the following puzzles to find x.

a $4 + x = 11$; $x = ?$

b $6 - x = 1$; $x = ?$

c $x + 6 = 9$; $x = ?$

d $9 - x = 7$; $x = ?$

e $x - 2 = 11$; $x = ?$

f $5 + x = 5$; $x = ?$

7 Each train carries 50 people.
  a How many people are in the carriage marked x?

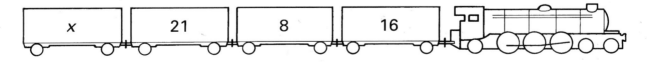

| x | 21 | 8 | 16 |

  b The two front carriages have the same number of people.
    How many are in each carriage?

| 10 | 18 | y | y |

Number Machines

The computer shop offers 2 free discs to each customer.

Jack buys 6 discs and gets the 2 free ones, making 8.

A number machine shows what happened.

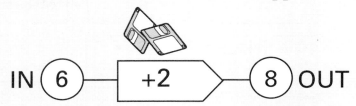

IN (6) —— [+2 > —— (8) OUT

6 goes in. The machine adds 2. 8 comes out.

EXERCISE 2

1 What comes out?

IN (8) —— [+2 > —— (?) OUT

8 goes in. The machine adds 2.

2 Work out the missing number in each case.

a
IN (4) —— [+2 > —— (?) OUT

b
IN (11) —— [+2 > —— (?) OUT

c
IN (16) —— [+2 > —— (?) OUT

d
IN (25) —— [+2 > —— (?) OUT

e
IN (?) —— [+2 > —— (9) OUT

f
IN (?) —— [+2 > —— (12) OUT

9 came out.
So what went in?

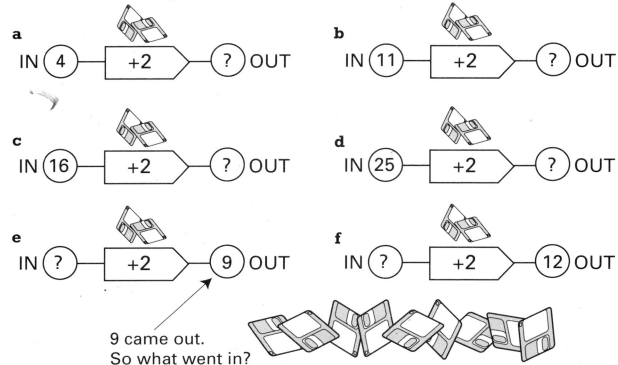

3 Different machines do different jobs.

For example, this machine adds 4

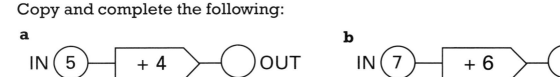

IN $\bigcirc$ — $+4$ — $\bigcirc$ OUT

and this machine subtracts 6.

IN $\bigcirc$ — -6 — $\bigcirc$ OUT

Copy and complete the following:

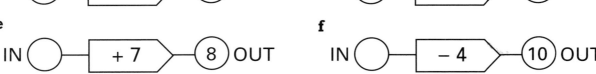

a
IN (5) — $+4$ — $\bigcirc$ OUT

b
IN (7) — $+6$ — $\bigcirc$ OUT

c
IN (9) — -3 — $\bigcirc$ OUT

d
IN (12) — -5 — $\bigcirc$ OUT

e
IN $\bigcirc$ — $+7$ — (8) OUT

f
IN $\bigcirc$ — -4 — (10) OUT

4 Copy and complete these machines.

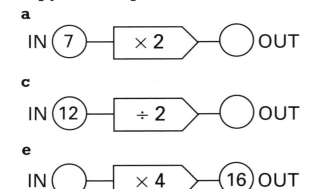
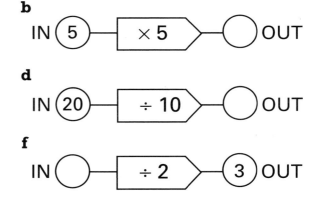

a
IN (7) — $\times 2$ — $\bigcirc$ OUT

b
IN (5) — $\times 5$ — $\bigcirc$ OUT

c
IN (12) — $\div 2$ — $\bigcirc$ OUT

d
IN (20) — $\div 10$ — $\bigcirc$ OUT

e
IN $\bigcirc$ — $\times 4$ — (16) OUT

f
IN $\bigcirc$ — $\div 2$ — (3) OUT

5 Copy and complete these machines.

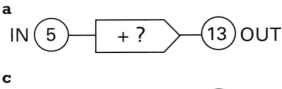
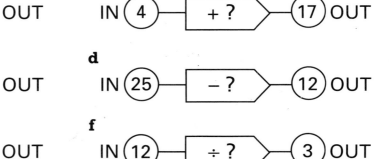

a
IN (5) — $+ ?$ — (13) OUT

b
IN (4) — $+ ?$ — (17) OUT

c
IN (8) — $- ?$ — (3) OUT

d
IN (25) — $- ?$ — (12) OUT

e
IN (4) — $\times ?$ — (12) OUT

f
IN (12) — $\div ?$ — (3) OUT

6 The same machine is used each time here.

IN   OUT

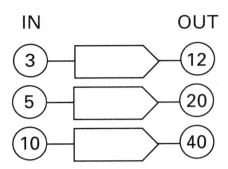

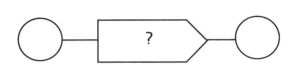

What does the machine do?

7 Which number machine should you place in each diagram?

You can only use each machine once.

a

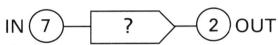

A

b

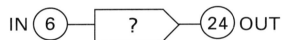

B

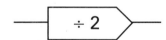

c

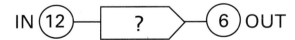

C

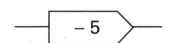

d

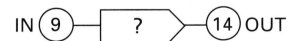

D

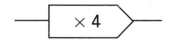

e

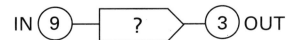

E

Coin Collections

Javaid empties his bank. He sorts the coins into types.

Javaid has [five] 2p coins.

Javaid has [5] × 2 pence.

EXERCISE 3

1 Copy and complete the following:

a Javaid has [   ] 5p coins.

Javaid has [   ] × 5 pence.

b Javaid has [   ] 10p coins.

Javaid has [   ] × 10 pence.

c Javaid has [   ] £1 coins.

Javaid has [   ] × £1

2 Find the missing numbers.

a   = [   ] × 10p

b = [   ] × 5p

c   = [   ] × 2p

d  = [   ] × £1

e 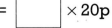 = [   ] × 20p

f  = [   ] × 1p and [   ] × 50p

g = [   ] × 2p and [   ] × 5p

The shop Suzie works in sells money banks.

Suzie puts coins in the banks to make them jingle.

She put 5 coins in the banks labelled *x*.

She writes down:

| $x = 5$ |

2 banks labelled *x*

2 lots of *x* means 2 lots of 5 $= \mathbf{2 \times 5}$
$= \mathbf{10}$ coins

She writes down:

| $2x = 10$ |

EXERCISE 3B

1 Copy and complete the following:

a 6 lots of *x* means ☐ × 5 = ☐ coins

| $6x =$ |

b 5 lots of *x* means ☐ × 5 = ☐ coins

| $5x =$ |

2 Copy and complete:

$$3x = \boxed{}$$

3  Suzie has 20 coins.
How many of these banks will she need?

4 Suzie puts 10 coins in the banks labelled y.

$$y = 10$$

Copy and complete:

a $2y = \boxed{}$

b $3y = \boxed{}$

5 Copy and complete:

a

b

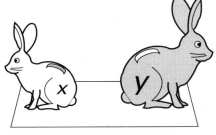

$$x + y = \boxed{}$$

$$2x + 3y = \boxed{}$$

CHECK-UP ON LETTERS AND NUMBERS

1 What are the missing numbers?

a

9   11   13   ?   17

b

26   28   ?   32   ?   36

2 What numbers go in each box?

a 4 + ☐ = 6   **b** 9 − 5 = ☐   **c** ☐ + 8 = 15

3 Score 20 with two darts and win a prize.

How much more is needed to win in each case?

a 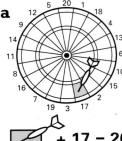   **b**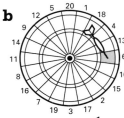

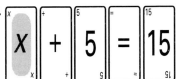 + 17 = 20   6 + = 20

4 What is the mystery card in each case? Find *x*.

a $x + 5 = 15$; $x = ?$ **b** $x - 8 = 12$; $x = ?$

c $x \times 4 = 16$; $x = ?$ **d** $x \div 7 = 2$; $x = ?$

5 Work out the missing number in each case.

a

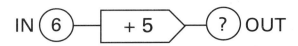
IN (6) — | + 5 > — (?) OUT

b

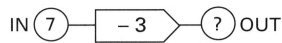
IN (7) — | − 3 > — (?) OUT

c

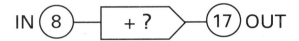
IN (?) — | + 4 > — (13) OUT

d

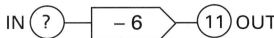
IN (?) — | − 6 > — (11) OUT

e

IN (8) — | + ? > — (17) OUT

f

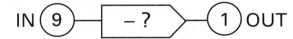
IN (9) — | − ? > — (1) OUT

6 Find the missing numbers.

a

 $= \boxed{} \times 2p$

b

 $= \boxed{} \times 20p$

c

       $= \boxed{} \times 1p$ and $\boxed{} \times 50p$

7 Suzie puts six coins in each of the piggy banks marked with an x. $\boxed{x = 6}$

Copy and complete:

a

 $2x = \boxed{}$

b

 $4x = \boxed{}$

Changing Money

 is the same as

 is the same as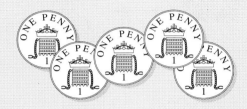

EXERCISE 1

1 How many one penny pieces can you change for these?

a

b

c

d

e

f

2 How many **five pence** pieces can you change for these?

a

b

c

d

e

f

3

Sam has  Sacha has  Together they have 35p.

Join these pairs in the same way.

a

Peter   Paul

Together Peter and Paul have ☐ .

b

Mary   Mandy

Together Mary and Mandy have ☐ .

c

Tariq   Terry

Together Tariq and Terry have ☐ .

4 James buys this: 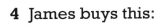 He gives the shopkeeper this:

The shopkeeper gives him 40 pence change.

a Bridget buys this:  She gives the shopkeeper this:

How much change should she get?

b Cindy buys this:  She gives the shopkeeper this:

How much change should she get?

c Graeme bought a magazine. He used a £1 coin.
The shopkeeper gave him this change:
How much was the magazine?

Pounds and Pence

Example 1 is worth  £1 = 100p

Example 2   250p is the same as £2 and 50p

Example 3   375p is the same as £3 and 75p

EXERCISE 2

1 How many £1 coins could you exchange for:

    a 200p **b** 600p **c** 400p **d** 700p **e** 500p?

2 Turn the following number of pence into pounds and pence:

  a 260p   **b** 320p   **c** 255p   **d** 352p **e** 456p
  f 458p   **g** 955p   **h** 881p   **i** 640p **j** 707p

3     70p + 50p = 120p = £1 and 20p

In a similar way, add the following.
Give your answers in pounds and pence.

  a 60p + 60p **b** 20p + 90p **c** 40p + 80p **d** 80p + 70p **e** 70p + 70p
  f 62p + 64p **g** 26p + 95p **h** 44p + 86p **i** 92p + 79p **j** 88p + 25p

4

Brian had lunch in a café. The starter cost £1 and 20p.
The main course cost £4 and 50p.
How much was the total bill?

5

£1 and 20p + £3 and 10p = £4 and 30p

Add the following in the same way:

a £3 and 40p + £5 and 20p   **b** £2 and 50p + £3 and 30p
c £4 and 60p + £5 and 30p   **d** £7 and 40p + £2 and 30p
e £2 and 80p + £6 and 10p   **f** £1 and 70p + £1 and 20p

£1 and 60p plus £1 and 40p gives £3

EXERCISE 2B

1 Add together the following amounts:

a £2 and 60p plus £3 and 40p   **b** £3 and 70p plus £5 and 30p
c £3 and 50p plus £3 and 50p   **d** £2 and 10p plus £3 and 90p
e £1 and 20p plus £3 and 80p   **f** £2 and 90p plus £1 and 10p

2 Add together: £1 and 60p plus £1 and 50p

3 Add:

a £2 and 60p plus £1 and 50p   **b** £3 and 70p plus £1 and 50p
c £3 and 60p plus £3 and 60p   **d** £1 and 80p plus £1 and 90p
e £1 and 25p plus £3 and 85p   **f** £5 and 90p plus £1 and 20p

4

	£	p
Starter	1	50
Main course	4	60
Total	6	10

Stacey got this bill at the café.

There is a column for the pounds and a column for the pence.

£1 and 50p plus   £4 and 60p

makes

£6 and 10p.

Work out these three bills. (You will find them on Worksheet 1.)

a

	£	p
Starter	1	60
Main course	5	50
Total		

b

	£	p
Starter	1	90
Main course	4	60
Total		

c

	£	p
Starter	1	50
Main course	6	70
Total		

Using a Calculator

£3 and 55p looks like this on the bills:

£	p
3	55

A line separates the pounds from the pence.

We can use the button on a calculator to separate them.

£3 and 55p looks like

```
3.55
```

and we usually write **£3.55**.

EXERCISE 3

1 £3.55 means £3 and 55p. What do the following mean?
  a £2.60   **b** £4.10   **c** £1.40   **d** £3.00
  e £5.30   **f** £1.00   **g** £0.50   **h** £0.01

2 Write out the following amounts.
  Use the point (.) to separate the pounds and the pence.
  a £2 and 35p   **b** £1 and 50p   **c** £8 and 15p   **d** £12 and 30p

3 Use a calculator and the button to add the following:

a

£	p
5	25
+ 3	50

b

£	p
2	30
+ 1	45

c

£	p
1	65
+ 0	80

d

£	p
2	48
+ 5	00

4

A Christmas novelty costs £4.95.

A card to send with it costs £1.20.

Use your calculator to find the cost of both together.

5 Jack's bill at the café came to £3.67.

What change does he get from a £5 note?

6 Fans of The Fang can buy T-shirts for £16.75. They can buy badges for £1.38.

Use a calculator to find:

a the cost of two badges

b the cost of a T-shirt and a badge together

c the change Tom gets when he buys a T-shirt using a £20 note.

CHECK-UP ON DECIMALS

1  How many one penny pieces can be exchanged for these three coins?

2 How much do Niall and Sandra have altogether?

Niall's money   Sandra's money

3 Janet buys a comic for 65p. How much change does she get from a pound?

4 How many £1 coins can be exchanged for:
a 500p   **b** 800p?

5 Add each pair of prices.
a 60p + 80p   **b** £2 and 40p + £1 and 30p   **c** £3 and 60p + £1 and 70p

6 Write each of the following in £ and p.
a £2.50   **b** £1.00   **c** £0.60

7 Write each calculator display in £ and p.

a 3.85   **b** 0.56   **c** 6.05

8 A poster for the gymkhana costs £2.25.

A badge costs £1.50.

What does it cost to buy both together?

Gymkhana

9 Michael's bus fare was £1.70.
How much change does he get from a £5 note?

5 FACTS, FIGURES AND GRAPHS

Sorting

EXERCISE 1

1 Jamie clears these tables in the restaurant.

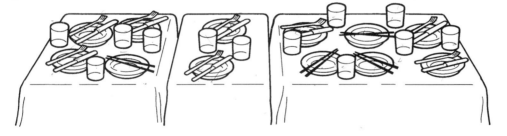

   a How many glasses does he clear away?

   b How many sets of knives and forks does he clear away?

   c Copy and complete this table.

	Item	Number
	Glasses	
	Sets of knives and forks	
	Bowls	
	Sets of chopsticks	

2 The next customers want take-aways. Here are their three orders.

3 Rice
3 Pork
1 Chicken

2 Chicken
1 Rice
1 Chips

1 Duck
2 Chips

Mr Kwan, the chef, wants to know how many of each dish to cook.

Copy and complete the table below to help him.

Item	Orders	Total
Rice	3 + 1 + 0	4
Chicken		
Pork		
Chips		
Duck		

3 More customers arrive and sit down at tables.
Jamie takes their orders for drinks.

TABLE 1
2 coke
1 orange
1 lemon

TABLE 2
1 apple juice
2 orange
1 coke
1 lemon

TABLE 3
1 apple juice
1 coke
1 orange

The barman sorts out the orders.

Copy and complete this table to help him.

Item	Orders	Total
Coke		
Orange		
Lemon		
Apple juice		

Mr Kwan does outside catering. He has made up all the meals for the Monday delivery.

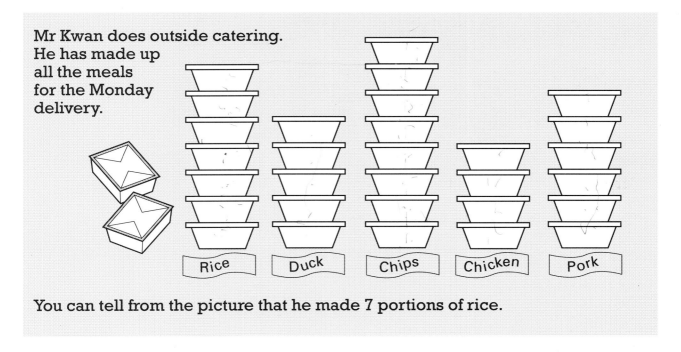

You can tell from the picture that he made 7 portions of rice.

EXERCISE 2

1 How many portions of duck did he make?

2 How many portions of chips did he make?

3 How many portions of chicken did he make?

4 How many *more* portions of rice did he make than chicken?

5 Which is the most popular dish on the order?

6 How many *more* portions of pork than duck did he make?

7 Here is a picture of Tuesday's delivery.

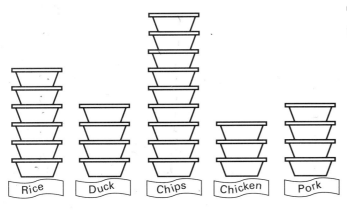

There is one less chicken ordered than on Monday.

a Which item has a bigger order than on Monday?

b What has happened to the pork order?

c Fewer rice portions have been ordered. How many fewer?

45

Here is Monday's order again.

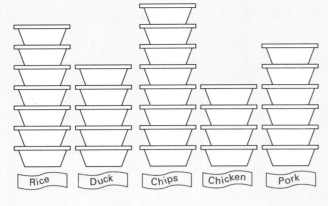

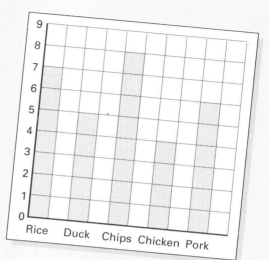

Mr Kwan made a bar graph of the
order for his records.

EXERCISE 2B

Here are some more orders.

(i) Wednesday   (ii) Thursday   (iii) Friday

Which of the above orders are shown by the bar graphs?

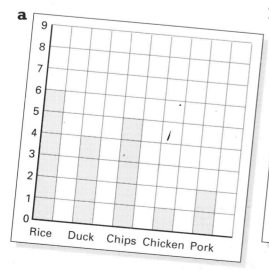

a

b

Do
Worksheet
2

Do
Worksheet
3

EXERCISE 3

Mr Kwan kept a record of how much petrol he used in his delivery van.
Here is a record from January to May.

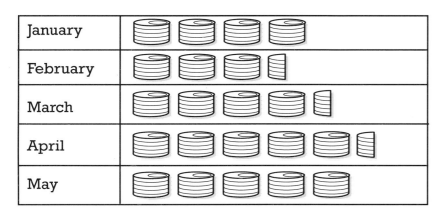

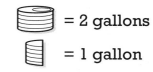
= 2 gallons

= 1 gallon

1 Copy the table and fill it in.

2 How much petrol did he use in January?

3 How much petrol did he use in February?

4 How much petrol did he use in the first three months of the year?

Month	Number of gallons used
January	8
February	
March	
April	
May	

5 In which month did he use the least amount of petrol?

6 How much petrol did he use altogether from January to May?

7 Draw a bar graph to show Mr Kwan's petrol record.

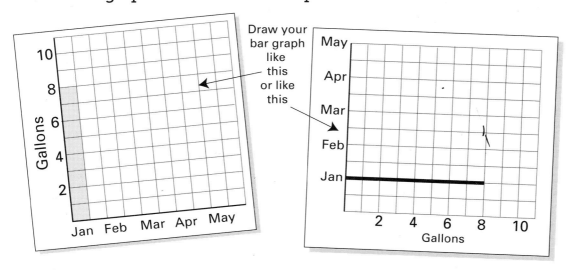

Draw your bar graph like this or like this

47

CHECK-UP ON FACTS, FIGURES AND GRAPHS

1 Jamie clears some more tables. List the number of items.

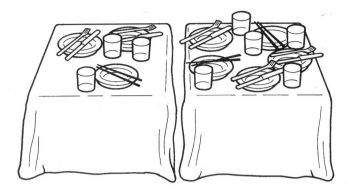

Item	Number
Glasses	
Sets of knives and forks	
Bowls	
Sets of chopsticks	

2 Here are the orders for one evening's take-aways.
Copy and complete the bar graph to show them.

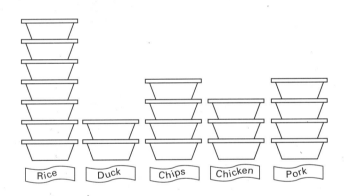

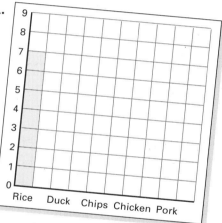

3 Here are Mr Kwan's orders one evening.

Dish	Tally
Rice	HHt
Duck	II
Chips	HHt III
Chicken	IIII
Pork	III

a How many dishes of rice did he sell?

b How many dishes of chicken did he sell?

c How many *more* dishes of chips than duck did he sell?

d What is the total number of orders for the evening?

6 MEASURING TIME

The Seasons

Winter, spring, summer and autumn - in which season would you send each card?

The Calendar

1 Which month will you see when you tear off March?

2 Which two months are still hidden on the calendar?

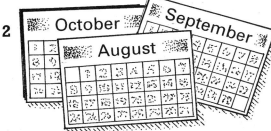

3 Now list all the months from January to December.

Ask for the game 'See You Later'.

The Days of the Week

It's a Date!

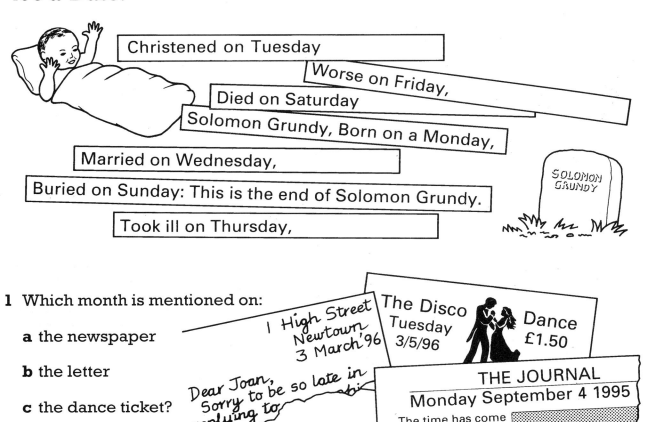

Christened on Tuesday

Worse on Friday,

Died on Saturday

Solomon Grundy, Born on a Monday,

Married on Wednesday,

Buried on Sunday: This is the end of Solomon Grundy.

Took ill on Thursday,

SOLOMON GRUNDY

1 Which month is mentioned on:

a the newspaper

b the letter

c the dance ticket?

1 High Street
Newtown
3 March '96

The Disco
Tuesday
3/5/96

Dance
£1.50

THE JOURNAL
Monday September 4 1995

The time has come
the walrus said to
talk of many things

Dear Joan,
Sorry to be so late in
replying to

2

This book is to be returned by:

05 07 96

The librarian sets the date on her stamp: the **5th** day of the **7th** month of the **96th** year.

The date is **the 5th of July 1996**.

What dates has she stamped here?

a   **b**   **c**   **d**   **e**

| 02 | 08 | 97 | | 06 | 02 | 99 | | 11 | 04 | 96 | | 22 | 05 | 97 | | 04 | 11 | 94 |

The Clock

This clock tells us that it is

2 o'clock.

This digital clock also tells us that it is

2 o'clock.

EXERCISE 1

Write down the time shown on each clock.

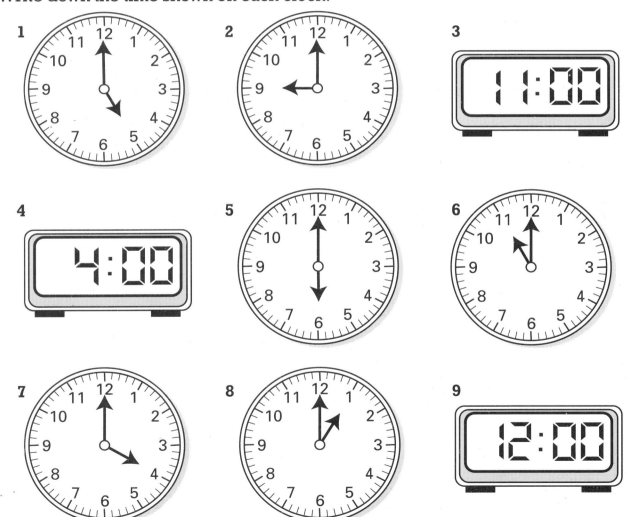

Past and To

On this clock the hand is not pointing to a number.
It has gone **past** the 1,
and is coming **to** the 2.

This hand is between the 7 and 8.
It has gone **past** the 7 and is
coming **to** the 8.

EXERCISE 2

On each of these clocks the hand lies between two numbers.

1 Write down which number the hand has gone **past** for each clock.

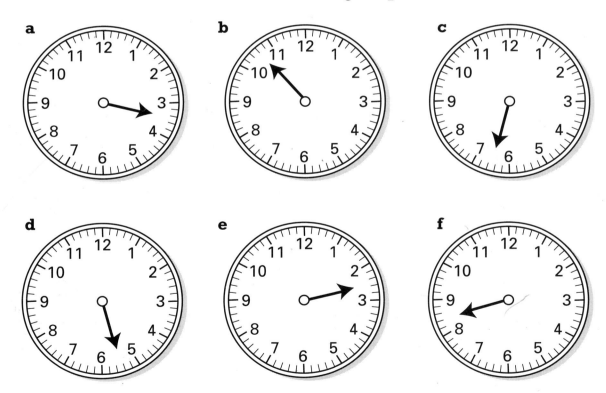

2 Look at the clocks again and write down the number that the hand
is coming **to**.

Half Past

When the **minute hand** has moved round from the 12 to the 6, it has gone 'half way' round the clock, so we say it is **half past** the hour.

The hour hand tells us which hour it has just gone **past**.

This clock shows **half past eight**.

The digital clock shows **'half past'** as **30 minutes**.

> 1 hour is made up of 60 minutes, so half an hour is 30 minutes.

This clock shows the time is **half past eight** as well.

EXERCISE 3

Write down the times shown on these clocks.

Ask to play 'Miss the Bus'.

Telling the Time

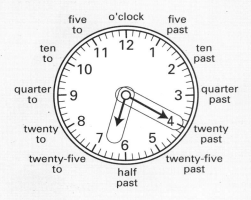

five to · o'clock · five past
ten to · ten past
quarter to · quarter past
twenty to · twenty past
twenty-five to · twenty-five past
half past

You will need a cut-out clock.

To tell this time:

a look at the 'longer' minute hand -
what does it say? (**twenty past**)

b look at the 'shorter' hour hand -
which hour has it gone **past**? (the **6**)

The time is **twenty past** 6.

To tell this time, follow the same steps and use your
cut-out clock to help.

a Set your clock to the same time as this one.

b Look at the minute hand. What is it pointing to?
(**five to**)

c Look at the hour hand. Which hour is it coming
to? (the **7**)

The time is **five to 7**.

EXERCISE 4

Write down the time on each of these clocks.

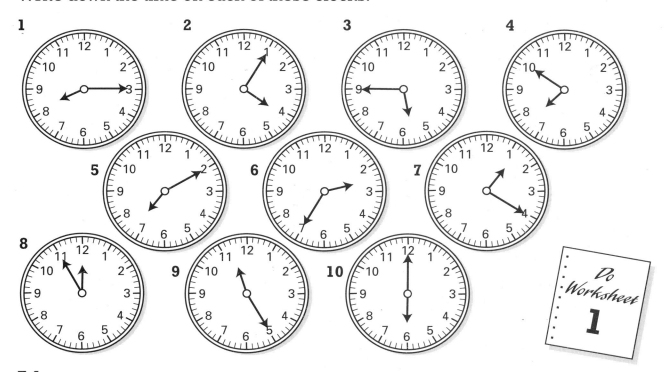

Do
Worksheet
1

Ask your teacher for 'Time Lotto'.

EXERCISE 5

	BBC 1		BBC 2
6.25	**Summer Praise:** Songs of praise from Galashiels.	6.30	**World's Islands:** Exploring Arran and the Cumbraes.
7.00	**Small Talk:** What the children have to say about it all.	7.20	**The Score:** Religious music and song.
7.30	**2 Point 4 Children:** How the average family don't behave.	8.00	**Under the Sun:** Where to go on holiday this year.
8.00	**The Tales of Para Handy:** Highland harbours and fishy tales.	8.50	**Monty Python's Flying Circus:** And now for something completely different.
8.50	**The News:** News and weather reports.		
9.05	**Antiques:** How your mother and father lived.	9.20	**The Quick:** What is going on in and around Kelso?
10.05	**Mastermind:** I've started so I'll finish.	10.20	**Grand Prix:** The Hungarian.

1  Which programme starts at this time?

2  **a** Which programme starts at this time?

b Which channel is it on?

3  At this time we have a choice. Name the two programmes.

4  Which programmes come after this time on BBC 1?

5 How long have I to wait for *Mastermind* to start?

am and pm

John has cereal for breakfast at 8 o'clock in the morning.

am means **before noon**

John has a roll for supper at 8 o'clock at night.

pm means **after noon**

EXERCISE 6

Which of the following are am times and which are pm times?

1  The morning papers arrive.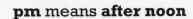

2  The evening news starts on TV.

3  Leave for school.

4  Have lunch.

5  Do homework.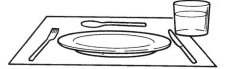

CHECK-UP ON TIME

1 In which **season** would you
send this card?

2 Which three months are still hidden on the calendar?

3 a Write this date in numbers only: 26th July 1997.
  b Write these dates using the name of the month: (i) 10/5/68 (ii) | 16 | 06 | 97 |

4 Write down the time shown on each of these clocks.

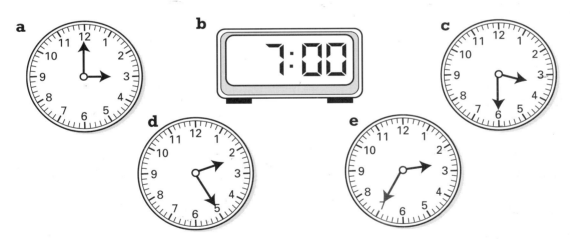

5

7.30	**Watching:** Mother comes home and makes the dinner.
8.00	**Wycliffe:** Victim suffers from poisoned tea.
9.00	**Framed:** Mother arrested for father's crimes.
11.00	**Evening News:** News and Weather
11.15	**Play for Today:** Arsenic and Old Lace.

a Which programme starts now?

b Which programme is on just now?

c Are these am or pm times?

Position and Movement

Miss Brown's pupils are on a biology outing to the seashore. They are scrambling about the rock pools collecting samples. Here is a picture of some of them.

EXERCISE 1

Write out the sentences below and fill in the blanks with one of these phrases:

| above | in front of | behind | to the left of | to the right of | below |

For example: Susan is **behind** Meena. Fiona is **to the right of** Jane.

1 Meena is .... Susan.

2 Philip is .... James.

3 Mark is .... Stuart.

4 Meena is .... Michael.

5 Stuart is .... Philip.

6 James is .... Mark.

Do Worksheet 1

EXERCISE 2

The class place mats on the beach where they can sit and study their finds.

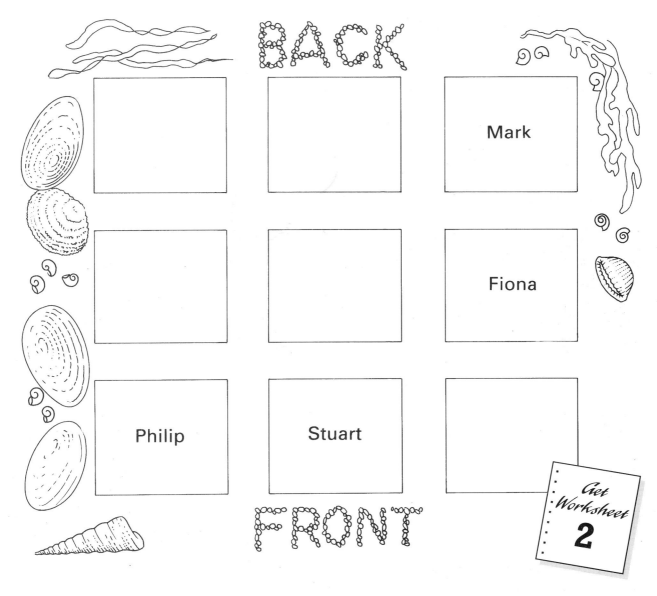

1 From the information below, can you find out where the other pupils are
   sitting? Write their names in the empty boxes on Worksheet 2.
   a Jane is sitting in front of Fiona.
   b Susan is sitting behind Philip.
   c Meena and Susan are sitting level with Fiona.
   d Michael is sitting behind Meena.
   e Susan is sitting in front of James.

2 Who is sitting in front of Meena?

3 Write down one way of describing where Mark is sitting.

Round the Clock

After lunch the children play a game at counting out round the picnic table.

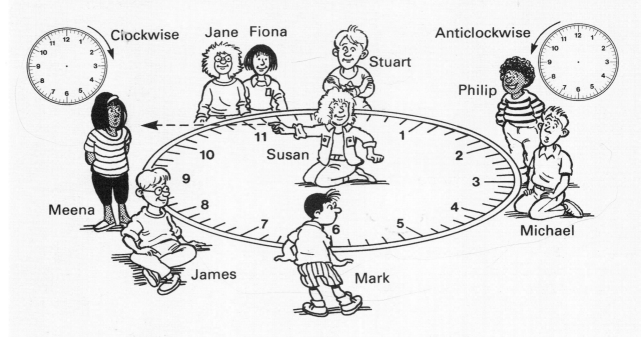

Susan points to Meena.

When Susan turns **clockwise** the first person she points to is Jane.

When Susan turns **anticlockwise** the second person she points to is Mark.

EXERCISE 3

1 Turning **clockwise**,
  a the **third** person Susan points to is ....
  b the **fifth** person Susan points to is ....

2 Turning **anticlockwise**,
  a the **first** person Susan points to is ....
  b the **fourth** person Susan points to is ....

3 Mark walks clockwise round the board.
  The **second** person he passes is ....

4 Susan makes a list of all the pupils. She starts with Meena
  and goes clockwise. Write down this list.

5 Mark walks anticlockwise round the board.
  The **second** person he passes is ....

A **whole turn** means a **turn through 360°**.

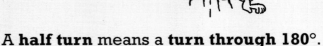

A **half turn** means a **turn through 180°**.

A **quarter turn** means a **turn through 90°**.

Ask your teacher for 'Round the Clock'.

The pupils play another game round the picnic table. This is how it works.
Susan points to one of her friends. She is blindfolded and turned, still pointing. Susan must guess at whom she is now pointing.

Example
Susan points to Meena. She makes a **quarter turn clockwise**. Susan now points to Stuart.

EXERCISE 4

Now try these (by setting the pointer on 'Round the Clock' and turning it).

Susan points to:

1 Stuart, and makes a **quarter turn clockwise**.
She is now pointing to ....

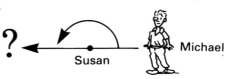

2 Meena, and makes a **quarter turn anticlockwise**.
She is now pointing to ....

3 Michael, and makes a **half turn**.
She is now pointing to ....

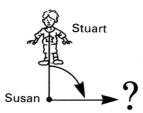

4 Jane and Fiona, and makes a **quarter turn clockwise**.
She is now pointing to ....

5 James, and makes a **half turn**.
She is now pointing to ....

Example

Susan points to Meena.
She is turned to point to Stuart.

She has turned a
quarter turn clockwise.

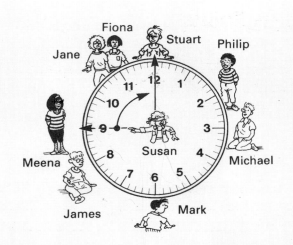

EXERCISE 4B

Now try these.

Susan points to:

1 Stuart, and is turned to point to Mark.

She has made a ....

2 Mark, and is turned to point to Meena.

She has made a ....

3 James, and is turned to point to Jane and Fiona.

She has made a ....

4 Michael, and is turned to point to Stuart.

She has made a ....

5 Philip, and is turned to point to Jane and Fiona.

She has made a ....

6 Michael, and is turned to point to Meena.

She has made a ....

Compass Points

The four main points of the compass are:
North, **South**, **East** and **West**.

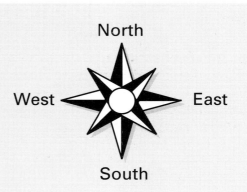

North

West — East

South

EXERCISE 5

On the bus trip into the seaside town, the pupils are given a puzzle sheet.
Follow the instructions to find the hidden words.

(F)			U							
							T			(T)
			N				(A)			
S		A								
		E			(S)			E		H
I				D						
				E						

Word 1
Start at the circled F.
Go East 3 paces.
Go South 2 paces.

Write down the word.

F __ __

Word 2
Start at the circled A.
Go North 1 pace.

Write down the word.

A __

Word 3
Start at the circled T.
Go South 3 paces.
Go West 2 paces.

Write down the word.

T __ __

Word 4
Start at the circled S.
Go West 4 paces. Go North 1 pace.
Go West 2 paces. Go South 2 paces.
Go East 4 paces. Go South 1 pace.

S __ __ __ __ __

Do Worksheet
3

EXERCISE 6

At the amusement arcade there is a competition to 'Win a Mystery Prize'.
The competitors do not know what is in each box.

For example, Jane picked B4 and won a bag of sweets.

	A	B	C	D	E
5	Beach ball	Pen knife	Sorry, try again.	Soft toy	£1 coin
4	Gift voucher (£5)	Bag of sweets	Cricket bat	Sorry, try again.	Story book
3	20p coin	Sorry, try again.	Watch	Sorry, try again.	Sorry, try again.
2	Toffee apple	Pen	Sorry, try again.	Phone card	Lunch voucher
1	Book of stamps	50p coin	10p coin	Sorry, try again.	Record token

1 What did each of these contestants win?
  a Philip, who picked box E1.
  b Meena, who picked box A4.
  c James, who picked box C2.
  d Stuart, who picked box A2.
  e Michael, who picked box D4.

2 Which box did each of the following choose?
  a Mark, who won the 10p coin.
  b Fiona, who won the pen.
  c Susan, who won the £1 coin.

3 Jane had another go.
  She did not win anything.
  Which boxes could she have chosen?

64

4 On the homeward bus trip, the pupils are given another puzzle sheet.

CAN YOU BREAK THE CODE?

	A	B	C	D	E	F	G	H	I	J
9		R		X		Y		Z		T
8	A			H		G			E	
7		K				A		D		L
6	C			S		B		O		
5		L		V				B		Y
4	R			I		F		P		
3		N		K			K			O
2		T					D		H	
1	H				V		M			N

Write down the letters in the named boxes to spell out the words.

For example, G2, J3, E1 and I8 spells out the word DOVE.

Now try these.

Word 1:   D6, D4, B5, E1, I8 and B9 spells   _ _ _ _ _ _

Word 2:   H5, I8, B5, B5 and D6 spells   _ _ _ _ _

Word 3:   F7, B3 and G2 spells   _ _ _

Word 4:   A6, J3, A6, C7, B5 and I8 spells   _ _ _ _ _ _

Word 5:   D6, A1, I8, B5, B5 and D6 spells   _ _ _ _ _ _

EXERCISE 7

1 While they were waiting for the bus, the pupils played a game on the paving slabs. They gave each other instructions to follow the shaded slabs.

For example:
Take 2 steps forward
Turn left
Take 2 steps forward
Turn right
Take 2 steps forward
Turn right
Take 3 steps forward
Turn left
Take 2 steps forward

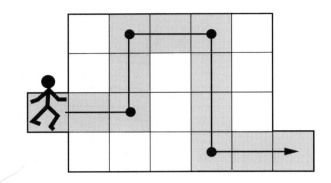

Write out instructions for each of these paths.

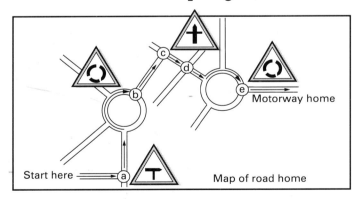

2 The bus driver used this map to get him onto the motorway home.

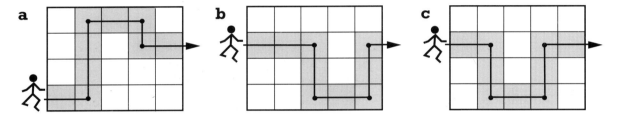

Follow the arrows to help you complete the instructions.

a At the first T-junction turn .... (**right** or **left**)

b At the first roundabout take the .... exit. (**first** or **second** or **third**)

c At the next T-junction turn .... (**right** or **left**)

d At the crossroads go .... (**right** or **left** or **straight across**)

e At the next roundabout take the .... exit. (**first** or **second** or **third**)

CHECK-UP ON COORDINATES

1 On the bus home some of the pupils sit in these seats.

Use the words

| to the right of | in front of | behind | to the left of |

to complete the sentences.

a Meena is sitting ………. Philip.
b Mark is sitting ………. Stuart.
c James is sitting ………. Susan.
d Fiona is sitting ………. Jane.

2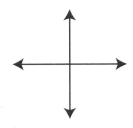

a Copy this cross and write down the compass points **North**, **South**, **East** and **West** at the correct arrowheads.

b Use the words

| a quarter turn anticlockwise | a half turn | a quarter turn clockwise |

to complete the sentences.

(i)   From West to North is a ……….

(ii) From South to North is a ……….

(iii) From West to South is a ……….

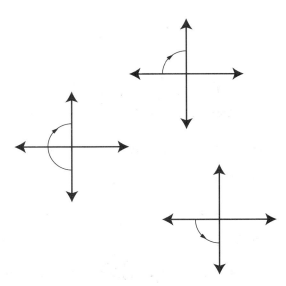

3 Here is a seating plan of the classroom.

    a Who is sitting in seat B2?

    b Who is sitting in seat A4?

    c Who is sitting in seat C3?

    d Which seat is Jane sitting in?

	A	B	C	D
4	Meena	Jane		
3		Fiona	Susan	
2		Philip	Stuart	Mark
1	James			

4 Write out the instructions to follow this pathway.

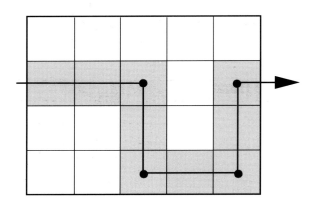

Right   Left

8 SOLVING EQUATIONS

Missing Numbers

Here is the control panel of a lift.

Some numbers have worn off.

We can work out what they should be.

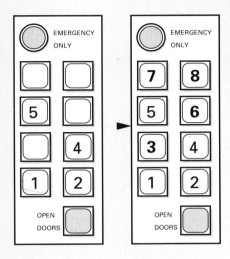

EXERCISE 1

1 What numbers are hidden by the thumbs?

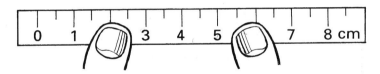

2 What numbers have worn away on:

    a the telephone   **b** the calculator?

3 What numbers are hidden by the pencil?

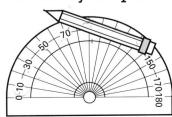

4 What numbers are hidden by the finger on the thermometer?

5 Look at the patterns.
What numbers are being hidden?

6 Each set of cards adds up to 10.
What is the value of the card turned over?

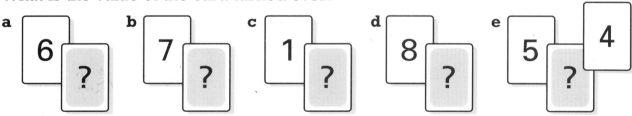

7 This time the cards add up to 8.
What is the value of the card turned over?

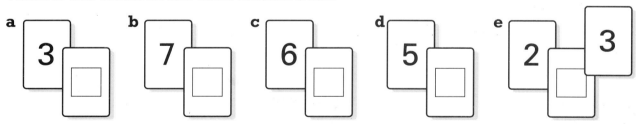

8 Now the cards add up to 16.
What is the value of the card turned over?

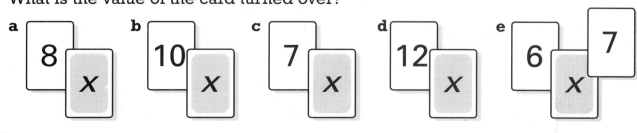

A number has been smudged by an inkblot.
What is the number?

The number must be 5
because 5 + 3 = 8.

EXERCISE 2

1 Ink has been spilled over Jan's homework.

Write out his work again for him.
Put in the blotted numbers.

a	$5 +$ ⬛ $= 8$	**e**	⬛ $- 5 = 2$
b	$1 +$ ⬛ $= 9$	**f**	⬛ $- 8 = 4$
c	⬛ $+ 2 = 8$	**g**	$10 -$ ⬛ $= 3$
d	⬛ $+ 7 = 8$	**h**	$12 -$ ⬛ $= 10$

2 Vijay and Jill play a guessing game.

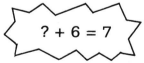 $- 2 = 6$

Vijay hides a number.

Jill works out
it's an 8 since
8 − 2 = 6.

$8 - 2 = 6$

Jill is correct.

Work out these puzzles for Jill.

a 🖐 + 6 = 10   **b** 🖐 + 9 = 11   **c** 7 + 🖐 = 15

d 🖐 − 4 = 6   **e** 🖐 − 3 = 0   **f** 12 − 🖐 = 11

3 Jill sees this puzzle in a book.   ? + 6 = 7

She hides the mystery number with her finger.

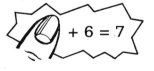 + 6 = 7

She writes   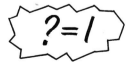 ? = 1

Solve these in the same way.

a ? + 6 = 8   **b** 7 + ? = 11   **c** ? + 2 = 2
d * − 2 = 4   **e** ? − 0 = 1   **f** * − 5 = 5
g ☐ + 7 = 10   **h** ☐ + 4 = 9   **i** ☐ − 10 = 11

4 *Example* There is money in the envelope. How much?

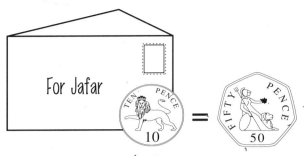

$+ 10 = 50$

$40 + 10 = 50$
so there is **40p** in the envelope.

How much money is in each envelope?

a

b

How much is in each envelope here?

5 How much is in each envelope here?

a 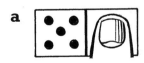 $+ 20 = 50$ **b** $+ 3 = 5$

c $+ 5 = 25$ **d** $+ 90 = 100$

e $+15 = 20$ **f** $+ 25 = 40$

6 A game of dominoes is finished.
Each player counts the spots on his last domino.

a 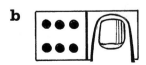 Paul says: I've a total of 9 spots.
How many spots are hidden?
$5 + ? = 9$

b Jack says: I've a total of 12 spots.
How many spots are hidden?
$6 + ? = 12$

c What is the hidden number for each of these?

(i) 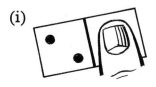   (ii) 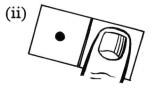   (iii)    (iv)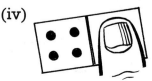

Balancing Act

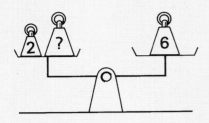

This scale balances,

so **2 + ? = 6**

The mystery weight must be 4.

(It helps to write: **2 + ? = 6**)

EXERCISE 3

1 **What must be put on the scales to make them balance?**

a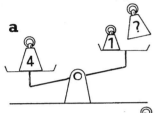

b

c

d

e

f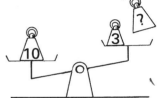

2 Each scale balances.
Find the mystery weight
in each picture.

Write it out as shown in
the example.

Example

3 + ? = 8

so **?** must be **5**.

a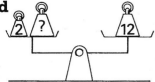

b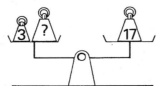

c

d

e

f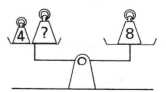

Equations

The apple weighs **3 + 1** units.

The apple weighs **4** units.

We form an **equation**

  apple = 3 + 1

and solve it.

  apple = 4

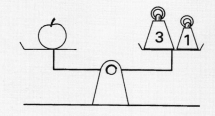

EXERCISE 3B

1 Form an equation for each balance.
Solve it to find the weight of each piece of fruit.

a Apple

b Orange
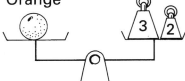

c Banana
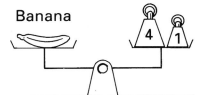

d Melon

e Pineapple
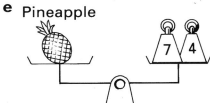

f Tangerine
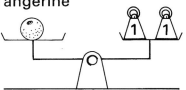

2 Form an equation for each
balance. Solve it to find the
weight of each piece of fruit.

Example

2 apples

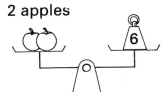

Form an equation:

2 apples = 6

so apple = 3

a 3 oranges
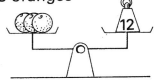

b 4 bananas
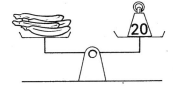

c 2 pineapples

d 5 tangerines
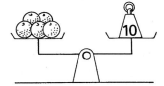

Problems

Equations can be used to solve puzzles.

Example
Nicki tapped out some keys
on her calculator.

What keys did she tap?

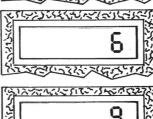

Form an equation: 3 + ? = 9

Cover up   3 + = 9   to solve the equation
and find the hidden key.   **? = 6**

EXERCISE 4

1 Here is some more key tapping.
Form an equation for each example.
Solve it to find the hidden key.

a + 2 =   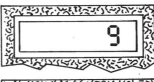 9

b − 3 =   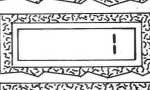 1

c 7 + =   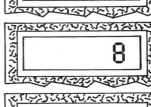 8

d 9 − =   6

e 3 3 =   9

2 We can use the **times** and **divide** buttons:

Solve each of these.

a   **20**

b   **3**

c   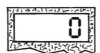 **0**

d   **12**

e    **12**

f    **7**

3 Think of a number!

a Samuel thought of a number.
He multiplied it by 3.
His answer was 12.

What was his number?

b Pat is 7 years old.
Suzy is twice as old.

How old is Suzy?

c The exam had 20 questions.
Ann got 3 wrong.

How many did she get right?

d The temperature goes up by 3°.
It is now 12°C.

What was it to start with?

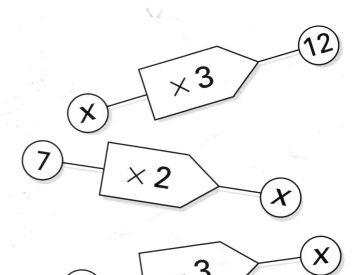

CHECK-UP ON EQUATIONS

1 Draw the TV controls and fill in the missing numbers.

2 What number is hidden?

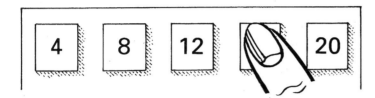

3 Each set of cards adds up to 12.
What is the value of the card turned over?

a
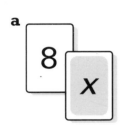

b
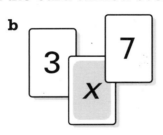

4 What number is smudged?

$$\text{✱} + 6 = 10$$

5 What is the hidden number?

$$\square + 4 = 11$$

6 How much money is in the envelope?

For Zarina

7 a Form an equation.
   b What is the mystery weight?

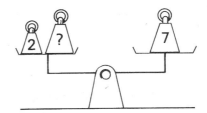

8 Form an equation.

Solve it to find the weight of one piece of fruit.

a

Orange

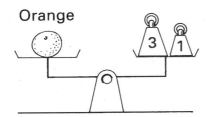

b 3 pineapples

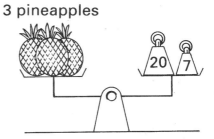

9 Form equations to find the hidden numbers.

a $\boxed{+}$ $\boxed{5}$ $\boxed{=}$ $\boxed{11}$

b $\boxed{-}$ $\boxed{4}$ $\boxed{=}$ $\boxed{5}$

c $\boxed{\times}$ $\boxed{6}$ $\boxed{=}$ $\boxed{18}$

d $\boxed{\div}$ $\boxed{2}$ $\boxed{=}$ $\boxed{4}$

9 MEASURING LENGTH

Here are some ways to measure length.

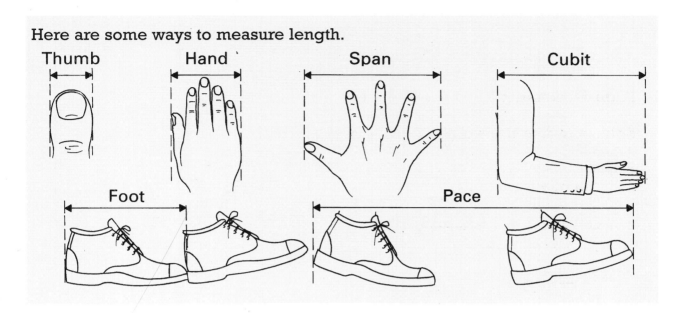

Thumb   Hand   Span   Cubit

Foot   Pace

EXERCISE 1

1 Use **thumbs** to measure. Record your results in a table like this.
   Guess the number of thumbs first.

What I measured in *thumbs*	My guess	Actual measure
Length of my jotter		
Length of my pencil		
Length of my desk top		
Height of my desk		

   Copy and complete this sentence: My guesses were ....

2 Measure some things in **hands**. Record your results in a table.
   Remember to guess first.

What I measured in *hands*	My guess	Actual measure
Length of my desk top		
Height of my desk		
Length of my leg		
Length of my ruler		

3 Use **spans**, **feet**, **cubits** and **paces** to measure some lengths.
Make a table for each one. Remember to guess first.

4 Find out:
  a how many spans make a cubit
  b how many feet make a pace
  c your height in hands.

5 Choose the *best* way to measure each distance:

  a the length of the football pitch
  b the length of my pencil
  c the height of the door
  d the length of the corridor
  e the thickness of the door
  f the distance to the school office
  g the height of a chair

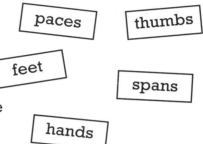

Do Worksheet 1

EXERCISE 2

1 a Which line is **longest**?
  b Which line is **shortest**?

(i)

(ii)

(iii)

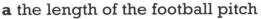

2 a Copy and complete these sentences.
  (i)   Mark is taller than ....
  (ii) Jack is shorter than ....
  (iii) Mark is shorter than ....
  (iv) The tallest boy is ....
  (v)   Jack is the .... boy.

  b Write the boys' names in order,
  with the **tallest** first.

Jack   David   Mark

3 Pupils in different classrooms
measured the distance to the
school office in **paces**.
They recorded their results
in a table.

Name	Distance in paces
Gemma	35
David	42
Kate	17
Ian	93
Robert	87
Mari	56

Assume all the paces were the same
length.
a Who travelled **furthest?**
b Who was **closest** to the office?
c Arrange the pupils in order.
Begin with the pupil who travelled
the **shortest** distance.

4 Horses are measured in **hands**.
Here is a list of horses.

Misty	15 hands
Silver	13 hands
Tansy	16 hands
Rocket	18 hands
Drum	14 hands
Smoke	12 hands

Record this information in a table.
Arrange the horses in order.
Begin with the **largest** horse.

PRACTICAL PROJECTS

1 Collect objects. Arrange them in order of:
length   thickness   depth   height.

2 Make a collection of coins. Arrange them in order.
Can you find different ways to do this?

3 Make a list of pupils in order of height.

4 Find out how many paces there are from your house to school.

5 Draw pictures to illustrate some of these words:
long   narrow   widest   highest   short   thin
wide   shallow   deep   lower   taller   tallest

EXERCISE 3

1 Collect a **metre stick**. Copy this table.
Look at the length and height of things around you.
Record as many items as you can in each column.
Don't use the metre stick.

More than 1 metre	Less than 1 metre
Height of the door	Length of my pencil

2 Find two things which measure about **1 metre**.

3 a Guess the **length** and **breadth** of the classroom in **metres**.
   Record your guesses in your jotter.
   b Now use the **metre stick** to measure. Record the actual measurements.
   c Work out the **total distance** round the room in **metres**.

4

Jane	48 m
Helen	39 m
Rashid	44 m
Joe	52 m
Karin	45 m
Andy	37 m

The list shows the results of a 'Welly throwing' competition.
The distances were measured in metres.

Copy and complete the table for the prizes.

Welly throwing	
1st prize	
2nd prize	
3rd prize	

5 Find the **total length** of each of these triple jumps.
Record the results in a table in order of length.
Begin with the **longest** jump.

Mary	
Hop	$1\frac{1}{2}$ m
Step	1 m
Jump	2 m

Fred	
Hop	1 m
Step	1 m
Jump	$1\frac{1}{2}$ m

Carrie	
Hop	$1\frac{1}{2}$ m
Step	1 m
Jump	$2\frac{1}{2}$ m

Jim	
Hop	$1\frac{1}{2}$ m
Step	1 m
Jump	$1\frac{1}{2}$ m

6 a How many centimetres are in $\frac{1}{2}$ metre?

b How many centimetres are in $\frac{1}{4}$ metre?

100 centimetres = 1 metre

Use a metre stick to help you find out.

Measuring in Centimetres

This line measures 10 centimetres.

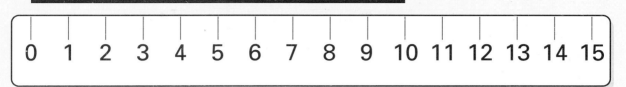

We can write **10 centimetres** as **10 cm**.

EXERCISE 4

1 Use your ruler.
   Measure the length of these lines to the **nearest centimetre**.

   a ————————————————

   b ——————————————————————————

   c ——————————

   d ———————————————————————

2 Draw a pencil which is exactly 14 cm long.

3 Measure the length and breadth of each of these rectangles.

   a

   b

   c

4 Draw a rectangle which is 15 cm long and 8 cm broad.

5 Write down the length of each key to the nearest centimetre.
Remember **cm** is short for **centimetre**.

a
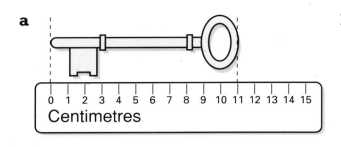

b
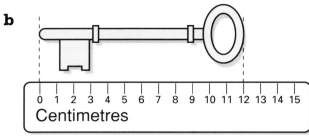

c
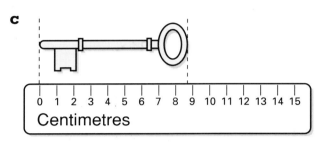

d
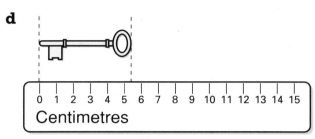

e
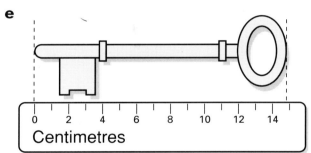

f
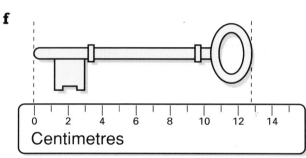

6 Draw a key which is 8 cm long.

7 Choose the best units (**metres** or **centimetres**)
for measuring these:
 a the length of the room
 b the length of your pencil
 c the length of a football pitch
 d the depth of a swimming pool
 e the breadth of your jotter
 f the distance round your wrist

Centimetres to Metres

Carol measures her height. She is exactly 134 centimetres tall.

Her height in **centimetres** is 134 cm.

Her height in **metres** is 1.34 m.

100 centimetres	=	1 metre
100 cm	=	1 m

EXERCISE 5

1 Write these lengths in **metres**.   Remember: 134 cm = 1.34 m

a 125 cm	**b** 234 cm	**c** 165 cm	**d** 332 cm
e 421 cm	**f** 389 cm	**g** 278 cm	**h** 108 cm

2 Write these lengths in **centimetres**.   Remember: 1.34 m = 134 cm

a 1.23 m	**b** 1.74 m	**c** 1.81 m	**d** 2.32 m
e 4.21 m	**f** 2.02 m	**g** 0.22 m	**h** 1.53 m

3 Copy this table.
Arrange the pupils in order of **height**.
Start with the **tallest** pupil.

Name	Height
Alan	1.35 m
Susan	1.24 m
Robert	1.31 m
Mike	1.29 m
Lucy	1.32 m
Kim	1.27 m

4 Jan has three pieces of wood.

58 cm long

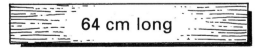
35 cm long   64 cm long

a Find the total length of wood in **centimetres**.
b Write the total length in **metres**.

Do Worksheet **4**

Do Worksheet **5**

CHECK-UP ON LENGTH

1 How many of your thumbs make a pencil length?

2 How many hands make the height of your desk?

3 Which line is longer?

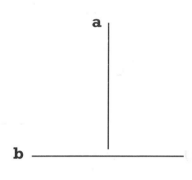

4 **a** Guess the length of the classroom in metres.
b Check it using a metre stick.

5 How many centimetres long is this toy car?

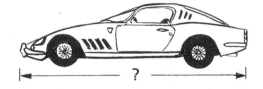

6 How many centimetres high is this model of the Statue of Liberty?

7 Remember: 257 cm equals 2.57 m
a Change the following measurements into metres:
(i) 349 cm   (ii) 718 cm

b Change the following measurements into centimetres:
(i) 8.65 m   (ii) 3.00 m

10 TILING AND SYMMETRY

Tiling

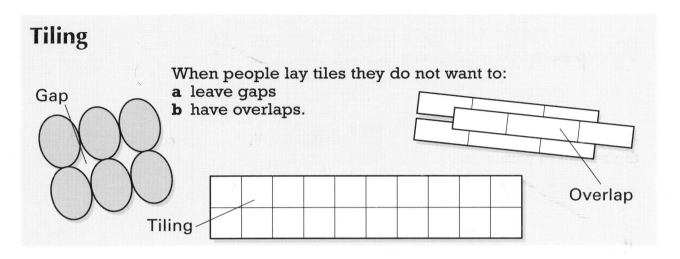

When people lay tiles they do not want to:
a leave gaps
b have overlaps.

Gap

Overlap

Tiling

EXERCISE 1

1

Katy's kitchen floor is tiled with black and white tiles.

a What shape is each tile?

b Are all the tiles the same size?

2 The kitchen wall is also tiled.

a What shape is each tile?

b Are all the tiles the same size?

3

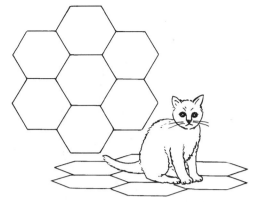

Cato the cat sits on the patio.
It is tiled with fancier shapes.

a What shape is each tile?

b Are all the tiles the same size?

c What would be awkward about using this shape for the kitchen floor?

Do Worksheet **1**

4 Denzil, Darren and Donna each design a patio for their garden.

They each choose a different shape of tile.

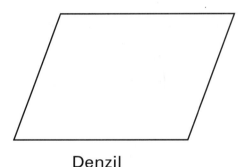

Denzil

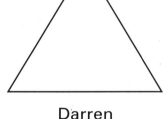

Darren

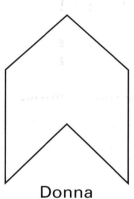

Donna

Complete each of their patio plans on Worksheet 2.

Get Worksheet **2**

5 David wants to use two shapes of tiles for his patio.

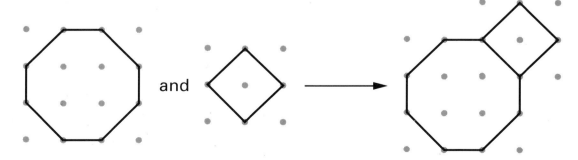

and

Use dotty paper to explore the sort of effect David might get.

Reflections

EXERCISE 2

You will need four templates, scissors, paper and a mirror.

Cut out a template.

Take a piece of paper and fold it in half.

Put the template on the fold and draw round it.

Cut out your shape.
(Keep the paper folded.)

Open out the shape.

Take a mirror and hold the template up to it.

What do you notice?

Repeat these steps for each template.

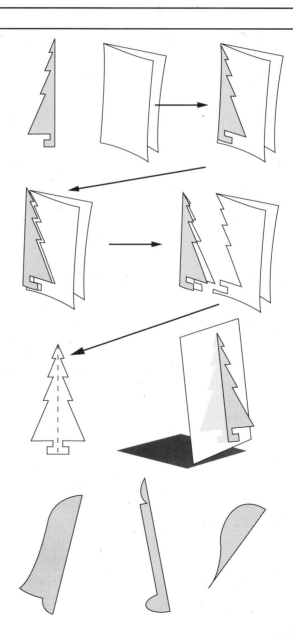

EXERCISE 3

You will need tracing paper and a mirror.
Trace each of these shapes.

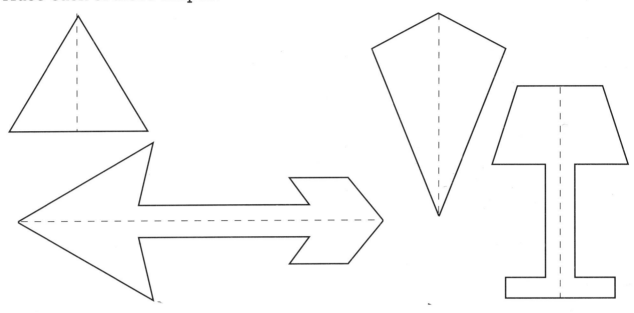

1 Fold each tracing along the dotted line.

What do you notice?

2 Place a mirror along the dotted line.

What do you notice?

The four shapes at the top of the page have one thing in common:
one half is the **mirror image** of the other.

We say: the shapes have **line symmetry**.

Examples showing lines of symmetry:

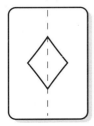

Do Worksheet 3

EXERCISE 4

1 Be careful! Some things are not what they seem.

The following figures do *not* have line symmetry.

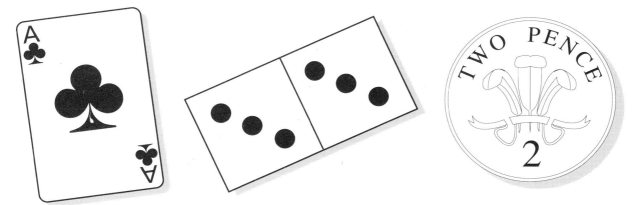

Use a mirror to check.

2 Some of these objects and words have line symmetry and some don't.

Use your mirror to find which *have* line symmetry.

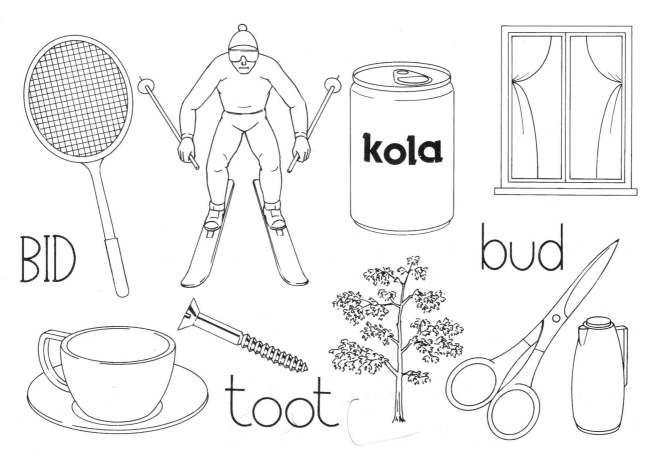

3 Gail thought that this photo of the kitchen window was symmetrical.

Find five things that spoil the symmetry.

Ask your teacher for 'Reflection Dominoes'.

EXERCISE 5

You will need dotty paper and a mirror.
If we know the line of symmetry, we can draw in the second half of the picture.

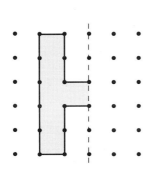 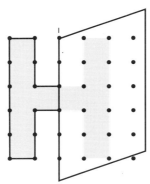 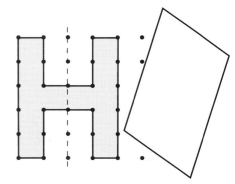

1 Draw this shape.

2 Put a mirror on the line of symmetry. Look at the reflection.

3 Draw the reflection.

Do Worksheet 4

CHECK-UP ON TILING AND SYMMETRY

1 Belinda's balcony is tiled with tiles like this:

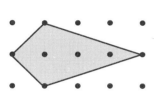

Copy this plan on square dotty paper.
Complete the tiling.

2 On square dotty paper explore how a **kite** tiles.

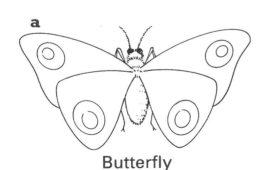

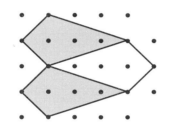

3 Trace each shape. Mark the line of symmetry.

a

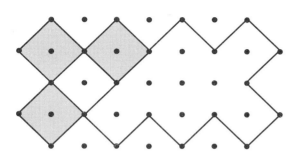

Butterfly

b

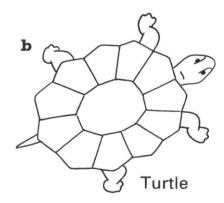

Turtle

c

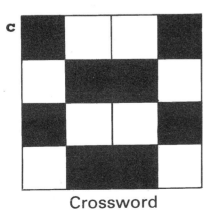

Crossword

d

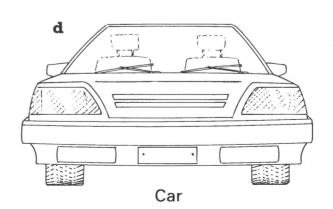

Car

4 Which of these shapes have line symmetry?

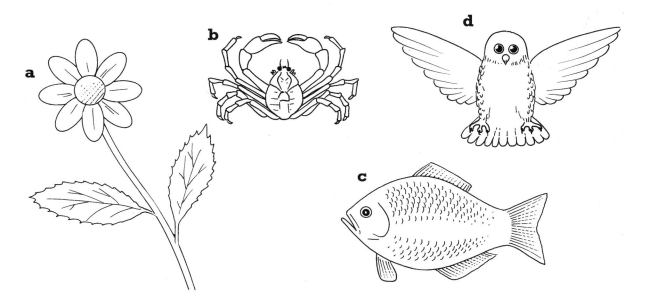

5 a Copy each diagram on square dotty paper.

b Draw the reflection to see the whole shape.

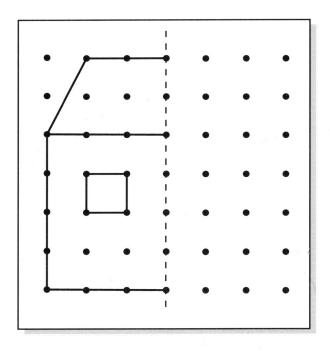

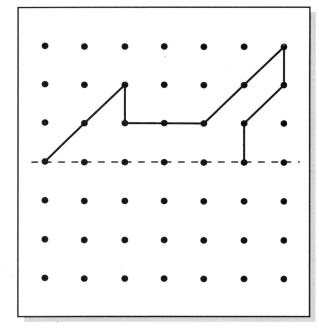

11 MEASURING AREA

Comparing Areas

Card B uses more card than Card A.

We say:
Card B has a larger **area** than Card A.

EXERCISE 1

1 Which of these cards has the largest area?

a

b

c

d

2 Which of the above cards has the smallest area?

3 Sort these postcards into order by area.
Begin with the largest area.

a

b

c

d

4 These shapes are made up of triangles.
We can find out how big each area is.
We can count the triangles.
Bigger areas use more triangles.

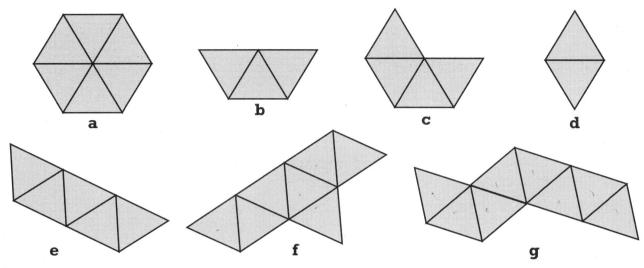

Record your results in a table.

Shape	Area measured in triangles
a	6 triangles
b	3 triangles
c	

Which shape has the largest area?
Which shape has the smallest area?

Do Worksheet **2**

5 Get some rectangular tiles.
Use them to measure the area of some other objects.
Guess the area in **rectangles** first. Record your results in a table.

What I measured	My guess	Area measured in rectangular tiles
Front cover of my jotter		
Front cover of my book		
Top of the desk		
Ruler		

This square measures 1 centimetre by 1 centimetre.

We call its area **1 square centimetre**.

This shape is made from 5 of these squares.

We say its area is **5 square centimetres**.

EXERCISE 2

1 These shapes have been made up of square centimetres.
  Find the area of each shape in square centimetres.

a

b

c

d

e

f

2 Look at these shapes.
  Guess which shape has the largest area.
  Guess which shape has the smallest area.

  Use a transparent grid to measure the
  area of each shape in square centimetres.

  How close were your guesses?

a

b

c

d

3

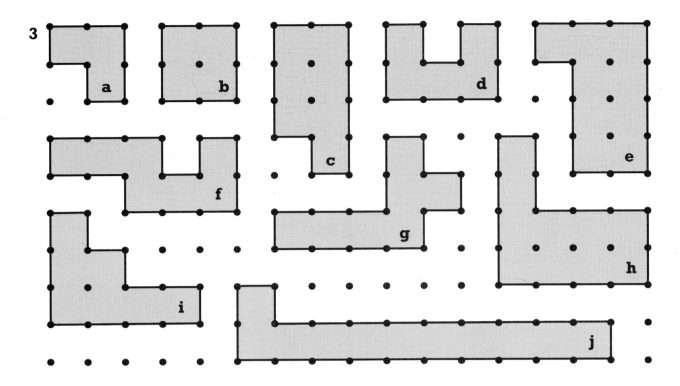

These shapes have been drawn on square centimetre dotty paper.

a Draw a table like this.

Find the area of each shape by counting the square centimetres.

Record your results in the table.

Shape	Area measured by counting square centimetres
a	3 square centimetres
b	

b Which four shapes have the same area?

c Which shape has the largest area?

4

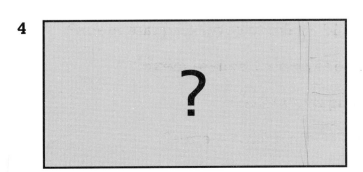

a Guess the area of this rectangle.

b Use a transparent grid to measure it accurately.

We do not use square centimetres to measure large areas.

Square centimetres are too small.

We can use square metres for large areas.

EXERCISE 3

1 Make a square metre.

    You will need: a metre stick
                      some large sheets of paper
                      sticky tape.

    Stick the sheets together.
    Trim the sides to make a
    square 1 metre by 1 metre.

2 Copy and continue the table.
    Find as many things as you can for each column.

Areas which are larger than 1 square metre	Areas which are smaller than 1 square metre
the ceiling	a jotter page

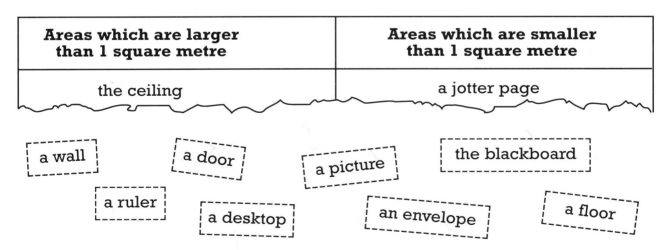

a wall   a door   a picture   the blackboard

a ruler   a desktop   an envelope   a floor

3 a How many square centimetres would it take to cover a square metre?

   b How many jotter pages does it take to cover 1 square metre?

   c How many people can stand on 1 square metre?

   d What is the area of the classroom floor in square metres?

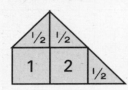

This shape has an area of $5\frac{1}{2}$ square centimetres.

This shape has an area of 3 square centimetres.

This shape has an area of $3\frac{1}{2}$ square centimetres.

EXERCISE 4

1 Find the areas of these shapes in square centimetres.
Count the squares and half squares.

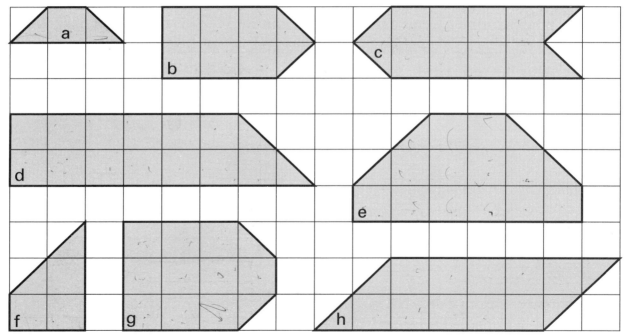

2 Make some shapes of your own on centimetre
squared paper.
Record the area of each one by counting squares
and half squares.

Do Worksheet **3**

Estimating Area

Some shapes don't follow the lines on the grid.

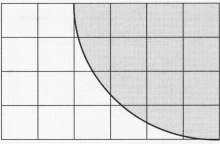

We can estimate the size by counting squares.

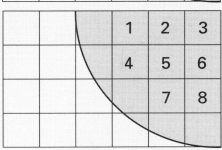

Count the whole square centimetres ...
and all the pieces which cover
half a square or more.

Don't count the smaller parts.

The area of this shape is about
13 square centimetres.

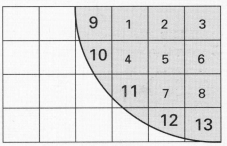

EXERCISE 5

1 Estimate the area of these shapes. Count squares.

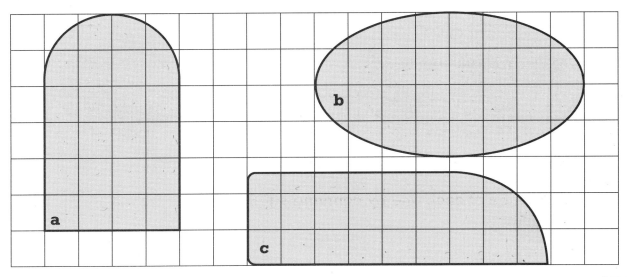

2 How big is your footprint?

Carefully draw round the sole
of your shoe on square
centimetre paper.

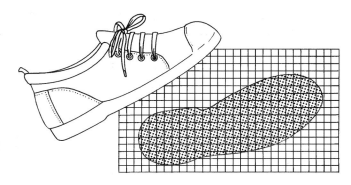

Estimate the area of your footprint
by counting squares.

3 Place these shapes in order of area.
Begin with the smallest. Do not measure the shapes.

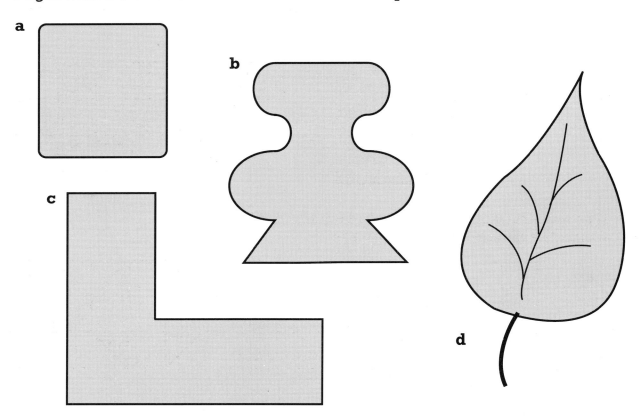

Now use a transparent square centimetre grid to help estimate the area
and check the order.

Remember: count whole squares and pieces which are a half or more.

Were your guesses correct?

CHECK-UP ON AREA

1 Place these stickers in order of area.
Begin with the largest.

a

b

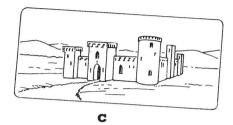
c

d

2 These shapes are made of square centimetres. Find the area of each shape.

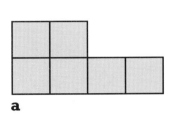
a

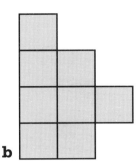
b

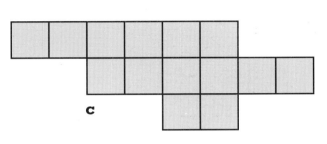
c

3 Find the areas of these shapes in square centimetres.
Count the squares and half squares.

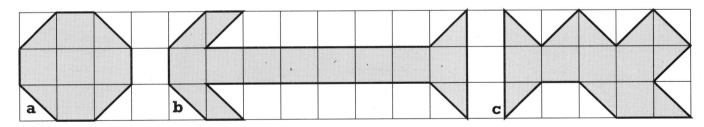

4 Which units would you use to measure these areas?

a the area of an envelope
b the area of the football pitch
c the area of the classroom floor
d the area of a sycamore leaf

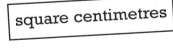
square centimetres

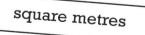
square metres

5 Estimate the area of this shape.
Count the squares.
Remember: half a square or more
counts as 1 square.

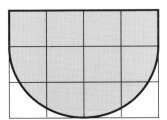

Patterns

EXERCISE 1

---

1 James is unrolling a roll of wallpaper.

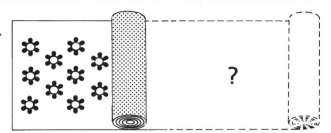

Which pattern will come next?

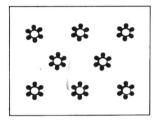

a

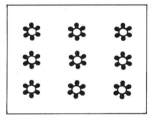

b

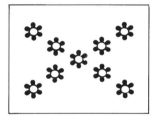

c

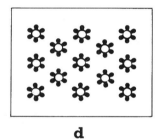

d

2

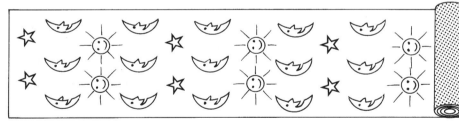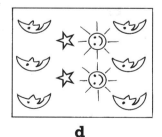

What comes next if we keep unrolling?

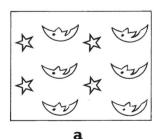

a

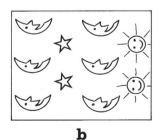

b

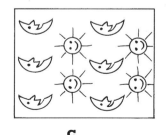

c

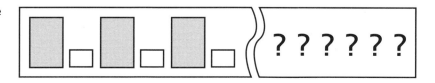

d

3 Copy and continue this pattern.

4 Copy this pattern and draw what comes next.

5 When you spot the pattern you can tell what is coming next.
Spot this pattern. What comes next?

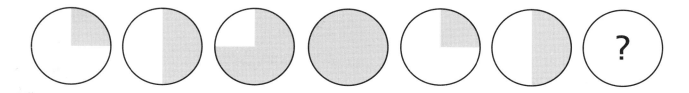

6 Copy and continue these patterns.

a

b

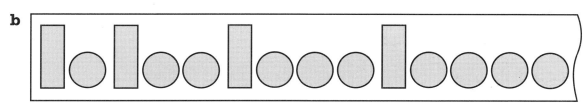

c

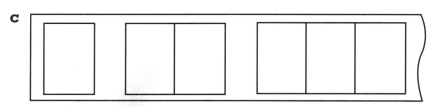

d

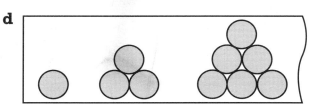

Number Patterns

We can make patterns with numbers.

2, 4, 6, 8, ..., ..., ...

This is an **adding on** pattern.

We begin at 2 and add on 2:

EXERCISE 2

1 This 'adding on 2' pattern begins at 1.

What numbers are missing?

2 This 'adding on 5' pattern begins at 1.

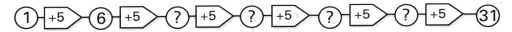

Write down the missing numbers.

3 Write down the missing numbers for each of these patterns.

a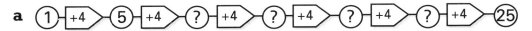

b

c

4 What is being added on each time?

5 What does *x* stand for?

6 a What does y stand for?

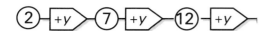

b 2, 7, 12, ... What comes after 12?

7 Copy and continue these 'adding on' patterns.

a +3 > 3, 6, 9, 12, ..., ..., ..., ..., ..., ..., ...

b +6 > 6, 12, 18, 24, ..., ..., ..., ..., ..., ..., ...,

c +4 > 4, 8, 12, 16, ..., ..., ..., ..., ..., ..., ...

8 This 'adding on 6' pattern begins at 40. Copy and continue it.

+6 > 40, 46, 52, 58, ..., ..., ..., ..., ..., ..., ...

9 Copy and continue these 'adding on' patterns.

a +3 > 16, 19, 22, 25, ..., ..., ..., ..., ..., ..., ...

b +6 > 23, 29, 35, 41, ..., ..., ..., ..., ..., ..., ...

c +8 > 17, 25, 33, 41, ..., ..., ..., ..., ..., ..., ...

d +9 > 20, 29, 38, 47, ..., ..., ..., ..., ..., ..., ...

10 Copy and continue these 'adding on' patterns.
Find out what is being added.

a +? > 34, 39, 44, 49, ..., ..., ..., ..., ..., ..., ...   ? =

b +x > 15, 24, 33, 42, ..., ..., ..., ..., ..., ..., ... x =

c +y > 12, 19, 26, 33, ..., ..., ..., ..., ..., ..., ... y =

EXERCISE 2B

1 Patterns follow a rule.
   a Copy these matchstick diagrams on square dotty paper.
   Draw the next two diagrams in the pattern.

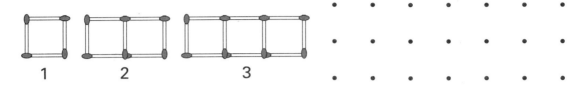

   1   2   3

   b Copy this table. Complete it by counting the matches in each diagram.

Diagram	1	2	3	4	5
Number of matches	4	7	10		

   c The number of matches makes an **'adding on'** pattern.
   How much is being added on each time?

2 a Copy these matchstick diagrams on dotty paper.
   Draw the next two diagrams in the pattern.

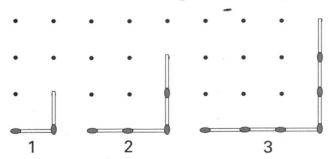

   1   2   3

   b Copy this table. Complete it by counting the matches in each diagram.

Diagram	1	2	3	4	5
Number of matches	2				

   c What rule can you use to find
   the number of matches?

3 Make some matchstick patterns
   of your own on dotty paper.
   Write down the rule for each pattern.

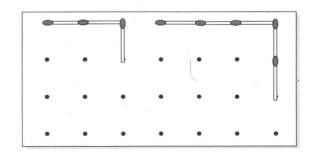

Number Machines

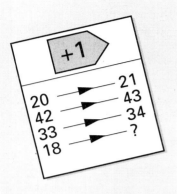

This is a **number machine** card.

It uses the rule ⟨+1⟩

So the missing number is 18 + 1 = 19.

EXERCISE 3

1 Write down the missing numbers on each card.

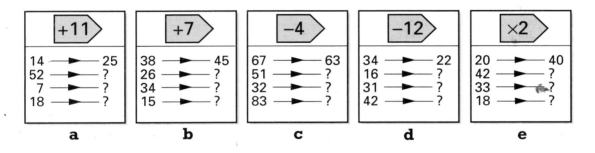

⟨+11⟩	⟨+7⟩	⟨−4⟩	⟨−12⟩	⟨×2⟩
14 → 25	38 → 45	67 → 63	34 → 22	20 → 40
52 → ?	26 → ?	51 → ?	16 → ?	42 → ?
7 → ?	34 → ?	32 → ?	31 → ?	33 → ?
18 → ?	15 → ?	83 → ?	42 → ?	18 → ?
a	**b**	**c**	**d**	**e**

2 Find the rule for each card.
(What numbers do x, a, t, y, ... stand for?)

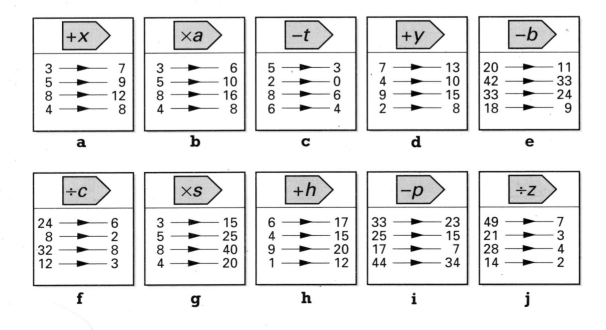

⟨+x⟩	⟨×a⟩	⟨−t⟩	⟨+y⟩	⟨−b⟩
3 → 7	3 → 6	5 → 3	7 → 13	20 → 11
5 → 9	5 → 10	2 → 0	4 → 10	42 → 33
8 → 12	8 → 16	8 → 6	9 → 15	33 → 24
4 → 8	4 → 8	6 → 4	2 → 8	18 → 9
a	**b**	**c**	**d**	**e**

⟨÷c⟩	⟨×s⟩	⟨+h⟩	⟨−p⟩	⟨÷z⟩
24 → 6	3 → 15	6 → 17	33 → 23	49 → 7
8 → 2	5 → 25	4 → 15	25 → 15	21 → 3
32 → 8	8 → 40	9 → 20	17 → 7	28 → 4
12 → 3	4 → 20	1 → 12	44 → 34	14 → 2
f	**g**	**h**	**i**	**j**

3 Number machine cards can be useful in spotting patterns and rules.

1 chick   2 chicks   3 chicks

a Copy and complete this table.

Number of chicks	1	2	3	4	5
Number of legs	2	4	6		

b What rule is on the number machine card?

c Use the rule to help you decide
how many legs there are on
12 chicks.

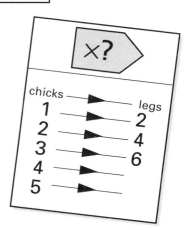

4

1 crab ... 10 legs   2 crabs ... 20 legs   3 crabs ...

a Copy and complete this table.

Number of crabs	1	2	3	4	5
Number of legs	10	20			

b What rule is on the number machine card?

c Use the rule to help you decide
how many legs there are on
12 crabs.

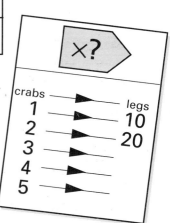

EXERCISE 4

1

1 bicycle   2 bicycles   3 bicycles

a Copy and complete this table.

Number of bicycles	1	2	3	4	5	6	7	8
Number of wheels	2	4						

b What rule can we use to find the number of wheels?

c How many wheels would 10 bicycles have?

2

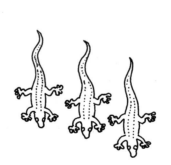

1 lizard   2 lizards   3 lizards   4 lizards

a Copy and complete this table.

Number of lizards	1	2	3	4	5	6	7	8
Number of legs	4							

b What rule can we use if we want to find the number of legs?

c How many legs would 10 lizards have?

3

 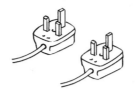 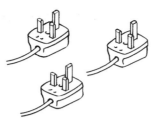 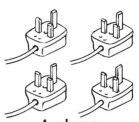

1 plug   2 plugs   3 plugs   4 plugs

a Copy and complete the table.

Number of plugs	1	2	3	4	5	6	7	8
Number of prongs	3	6						

b What rule can we use if we want to know how many prongs?

c How many prongs would there be for 9 plugs?

4

1 foot   2 feet   3 feet

a Copy and complete the table.

Number of feet	1	2	3	4	5	6	7	8
Number of toes								

b What rule can we use if we want to know how many toes?

c How many toes would 10 feet have?

d How many toes would 20 feet have?

5 Describe some patterns of your own and make up a table about them.

6 Play the 'Sequence Game'.

CHECK-UP ON LETTERS, NUMBERS AND SEQUENCES

1 Complete the 'adding on' patterns.

a | +8 ⟩   15, 23, 31, 39, ..., ..., ..., ..., ..., ..., ...

b | +6 ⟩   13, 19, 25, 31, ..., ..., ..., ..., ..., ..., ...

2 Complete the pattern and find what the letters stand for.

a | +b ⟩   29, 38, 47, 56, ..., ..., ..., ..., ..., ..., ... | b = |

b | −c ⟩   66, 62, 58, 54, ..., ..., ..., ..., ..., ..., ... | c = |

3 The rule for each pattern has been written using letters.
What numbers do the letters stand for?

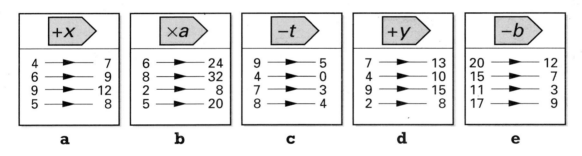

+x ⟩		×a ⟩		−t ⟩		+y ⟩		−b ⟩
4 → 7		6 → 24		9 → 5		7 → 13		20 → 12
6 → 9		8 → 32		4 → 0		4 → 10		15 → 7
9 → 12		2 → 8		7 → 3		9 → 15		11 → 3
5 → 8		5 → 20		8 → 4		2 → 8		17 → 9
a		**b**		**c**		**d**		**e**

4

1 frog   2 frogs   3 frogs

a Copy and complete the table.

Number of frogs	1	2	3	4	5	6	7	8
Number of legs	4							

b What rule can we use if we want to know how many legs?

c How many legs would 10 frogs have?

d How many legs would 12 frogs have?

13 TWO DIMENSIONS

Naming Shapes

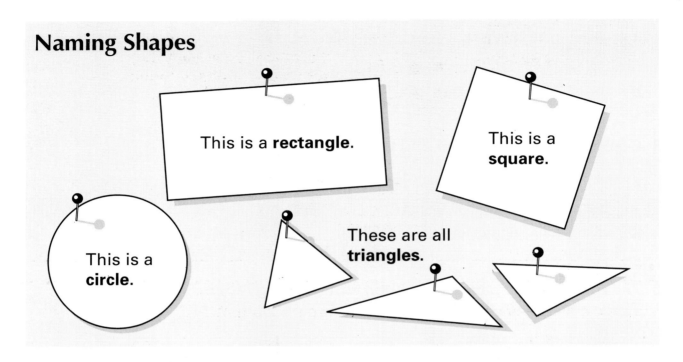

This is a **rectangle**.

This is a **square**.

This is a **circle**.

These are all **triangles**.

EXERCISE 1

Write down the names of the following shapes.

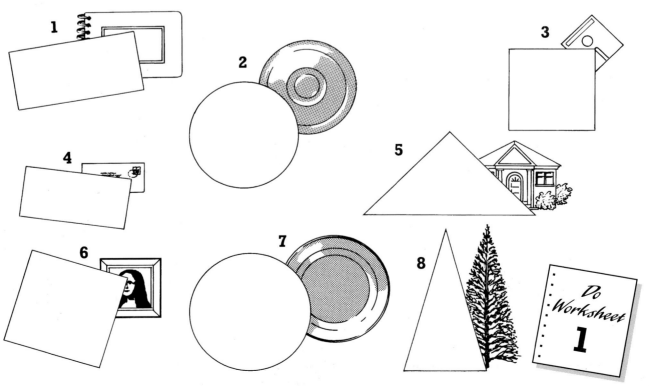

Do Worksheet 1

Faces

The dice has 6 faces.
Each face is a **square**.
This face is a square.

This face is a square too, although it does not look like it.

Each face of the shoebox is a **rectangle**.

EXERCISE 2

Name the shape of each face the arrows are pointing at.

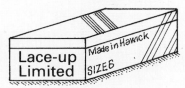

Now ask to play 'Shapes Galore'.

The Rectangle

The rectangle has:
two pairs of equal sides
a right angle at each corner.

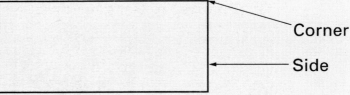

Corner

Side

Look at how we mark the
diagram to show this.

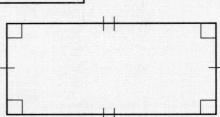

The Square

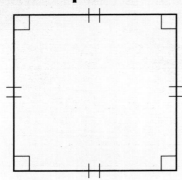

The four sides of the square are equal in length.

The four corners of the square are all right angles.

Look at how we mark the diagram to show this.

EXERCISE 3

You will need centimetre square paper.
1 Draw a 5 centimetre by 5 centimetre square.
  Mark on it the equal sides and the right angles.

2 Draw a 6 centimetre by 4 centimetre rectangle.
  Mark on it the equal sides and the right angles.

3 What is wrong with the way
  this diagram is marked?

4 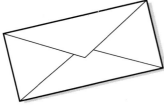 This airmail envelope is a rectangle which
  is 10 cm by 5 cm.
  a Draw the front of the envelope on squared paper.
  b The stamp on the envelope is 2 cm by 2 cm square.
  Draw the square for the stamp on your envelope.

Labelling Shapes

Here are two rectangles. To tell them apart we have labelled them.

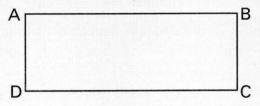

This is rectangle ABCD.   This is rectangle EFGH.

It is important to mention the letters in the order you meet them when drawing.

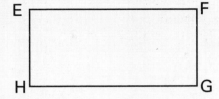

Here we draw the rectangle PQRS.   Here we draw the bow-tie PSQR.

EXERCISE 4

1 Name the three rectangles.

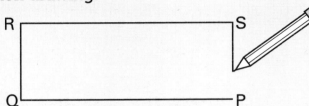
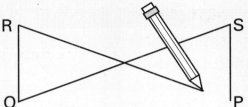

2 Name the three squares.

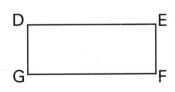

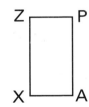

3 a Make four copies of these dots.
   b Join them up in the following orders:
   (i) ABCD   (ii) ADBC
 (iii) ACDB   (iv) ACBD
   Finish each drawing to point A.
   c Which of these give rectangles?

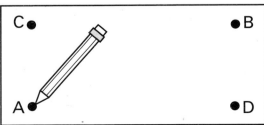

CHECK-UP ON TWO DIMENSIONS

1 Name each of these shapes.

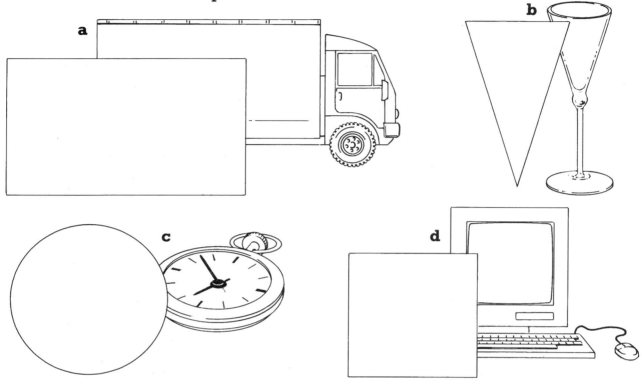

2 Name the faces marked with the arrows.

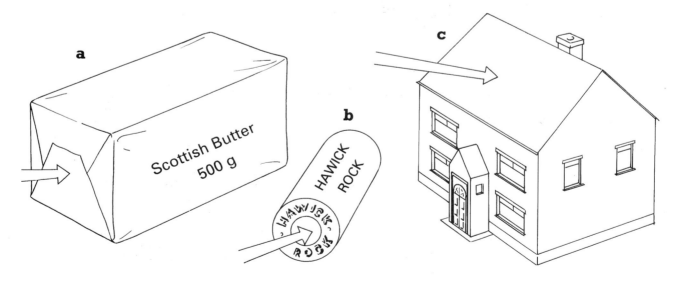

3 Draw a rectangle 4 cm by 5 cm on squared paper. Mark on it:
   a the equal sides
   b the right angles.

14 MEASURING VOLUME

Comparing Sizes

EXERCISE 1

1 Which holds more water when it is full, a sink or a bath?

2 Which takes up more space, a box of cornflakes or a pack of butter?

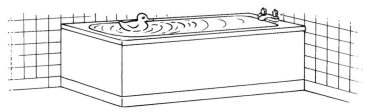 

3 Put these in order. Start with the one which holds the most.

an egg cup   a kettle   a tea cup

4 Put these in order. Start with the one that takes up most space in real life.

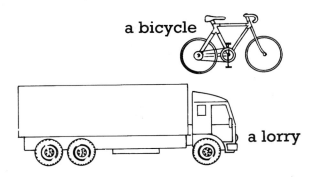 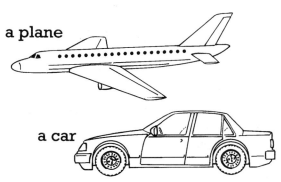

a bicycle   a plane   a lorry   a car

EXERCISE 2

Here is part of an Australian recipe for sultana scones.

You will need: 2 cups self-raising flour
1 half teaspoon salt
2 teaspoons sugar
1 heaped tablespoon butter
Half cup milk
Quarter cup water
Small handful of sultanas

The ingredients make 10 scones.

Look at the ingredients listed above and answer these questions.

1 How much flour does the recipe use?

2 What do we use to measure out the sugar?

3 Does the recipe use more water or more milk?

4 This recipe is for 10 scones. Ewan wants to make 40 scones.
How much sugar will he need to put in?

5 A bag of flour contains 12 cupfuls.
a How many batches of scones could Ewan make from this bag?
b How many scones would he have if he used up all the flour?

EXERCISE 3

1  The doctor told Joanna to take 6 spoonfuls
of medicine every day.
The bottle holds 42 spoonfuls.
For how many days will Joanna have to take
her medicine?

2 This can of soup holds 5 ladlefuls.
Rachel has 2 ladlefuls.
Sandy has 1 ladleful.
How much is left for Catriona?

3  This large tin holds 6 ladlefuls.
To make up the soup, you add
the same amount of water.
How many ladlefuls of soup
would you have altogether?

When we buy things we want to know exactly how much we are getting.
Liquids are usually sold in **litres** or **pints**.

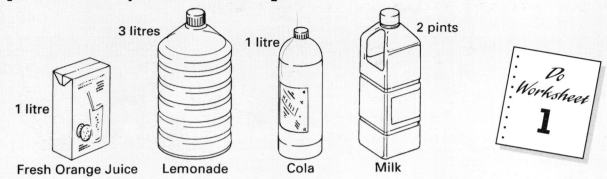

3 litres — Lemonade
1 litre — Cola
2 pints — Milk
1 litre — Fresh Orange Juice
Do Worksheet 1

EXERCISE 4

1 Each beaker is marked in litres.
How many litres of coloured water are in each?

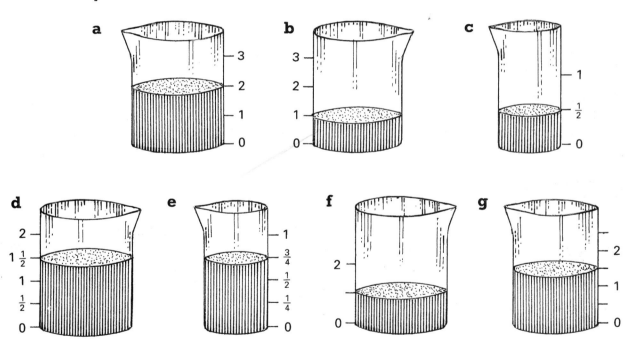

2 A container of milk holds 2 litres.
The Hillerton family drink half a litre at dinner time.
How much milk is left?

3 A large bottle of cola holds 1 litre.
Each glass holds half a litre.
How many glasses can be filled from the bottle?

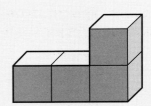

This is a picture of 1 cube.

Each side is a centimetre.
We call it a cubic centimetre.

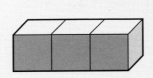

This solid shape is made of 3 cubic centimetres.

This solid shape is made of 4 cubic centimetres.

EXERCISE 5

How many cubic centimetres are needed to make each of these solid shapes?

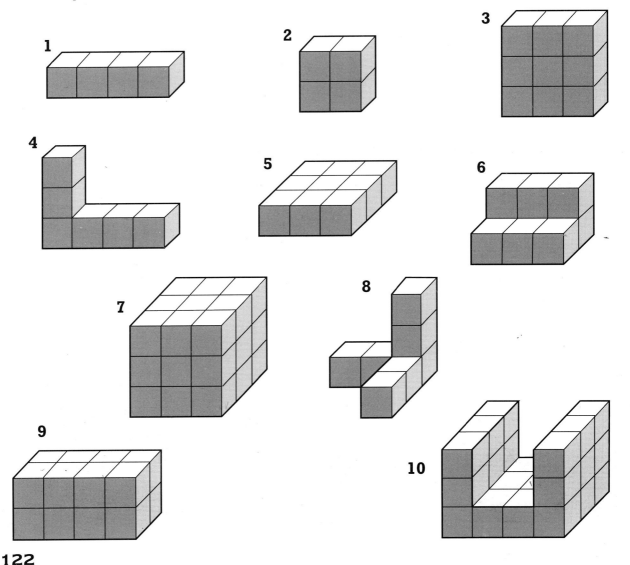

The amount of space something takes up is called its **volume**.
One volume is bigger than another if it takes up more
space.

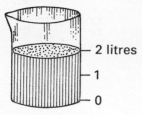

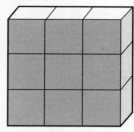

The volume of water in
this beaker is 2 litres.

This solid has a volume
of 9 cubic centimetres.

EXERCISE 6

1 Which has the bigger volume, the carton of milk or the carton of juice?

Milk
1 litre

Orange juice

$\frac{1}{2}$ litre

2 Write down the volume of coloured water in each container.

a

3 litres

2

1

0

b

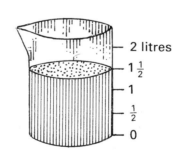

2 litres

$1\frac{1}{2}$

1

$\frac{1}{2}$

0

3 Which of these solids has the largest volume?

a

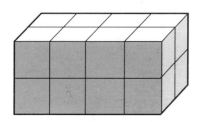

b

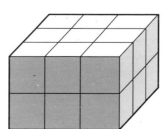

c

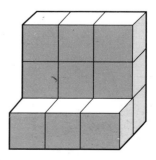

CHECK-UP ON VOLUME

1 In real life, which takes up more space, an elephant or a rabbit?

2 Which has a bigger volume, a train or a car?

3 Which of these contains the bigger volume of orange juice?

a

— 2 litres
— 1
— 0

b

Sunshine Orange Juice
1 litre

4 a How many cubic centimetres are needed to make these shapes?

(i) (ii) (iii)

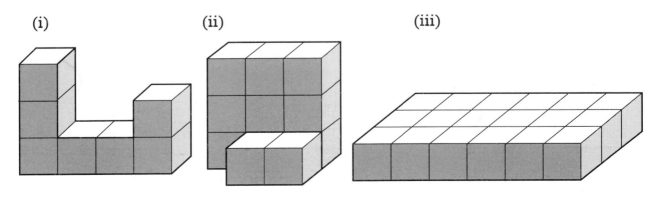

b Which of them has the smallest volume?

15 FRACTIONS

Equal Parts

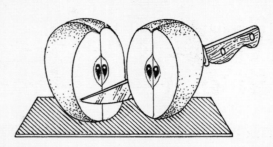

An apple is cut into two equal parts.
Andrea gets one of the two parts.
We say Andrea gets half.

EXERCISE 1

1 Which line cuts the chocolate bar into two equal parts?

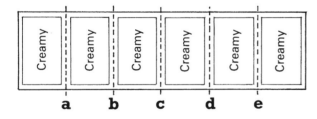

2 Who is standing on the line which cuts the pitch in half?

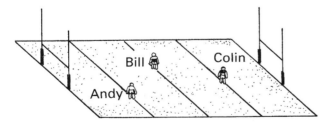

3 Which jug is half full?

4 Which of these show halves?
Remember: we must have two equal parts.

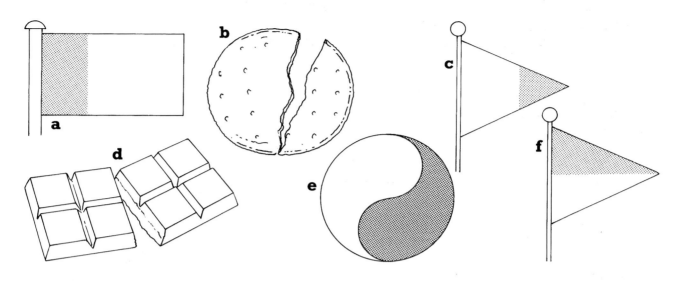

The cake is cut into two equal parts.
Each part is a half of the cake.

We write: $\frac{1}{2}$ meaning 1 part out of 2.

This cake is cut into three equal parts.
Each part is a third of the cake.

We write: $\frac{1}{3}$ meaning 1 part out of 3.

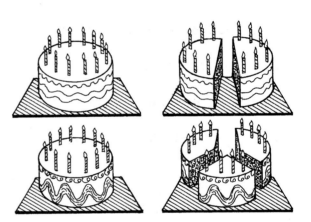

EXERCISE 2

1 a

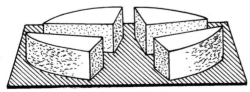

Four equal parts.
Each part is a quarter of the cake.
Copy and complete:

$\frac{1}{\boxed{}}$ means 1 part out of $\boxed{}$

b

Five equal parts.
Each part is a fifth of the cake.
Copy and complete:

$\frac{1}{\boxed{}}$ means 1 part out of $\boxed{}$

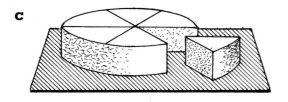

c

Six equal parts.
Each part is a sixth of the cake.
Copy and complete:

$\dfrac{1}{\boxed{}}$ means 1 part out of $\boxed{}$

2 Write similar statements for:
   a sevenths   **b** eighths   **c** ninths.

3 Ask for a sheet of shape cards and scissors.

   a Cut a shape out.

   b Cut it up along the dotted lines.

   c Glue the pieces into your jotter.

   d Colour one piece.

   e Name the piece and write it as a fraction.

   f Do this with all the shapes.

4 A stick of rock is divided equally amongst five people.

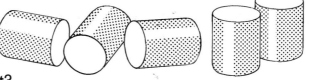

   What fraction does each person get?

5

This bar of chocolate is split into squares.

   a How many squares are there?
   b What fraction of the bar is one square?

6 This block of ice-cream is made of equal layers of chocolate, vanilla and mint.

   What fraction is vanilla?

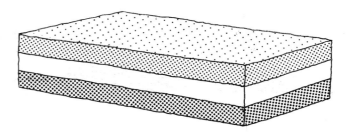

7 I cut a pie into eighths.
How many pieces do I get?

8 A pizza is shared amongst nine people.
What fraction does each get?

9 a Which is bigger:
    (i) a half or a quarter
   (ii) a quarter or a third
  (iii) a half or a third?

b Which jug is

(i) $\frac{1}{2}$ full   (ii) $\frac{1}{4}$ full 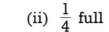   (iii) $\frac{1}{3}$ full?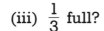

Hassan took a quarter of the cake.

He left three quarters for his friends.

Three quarters means **3** parts out of **4**

and is written: $\frac{3}{4}$

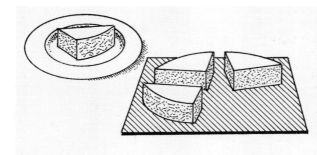

EXERCISE 3

1 Emma took a fifth of this cake.
What fraction is left for the others?

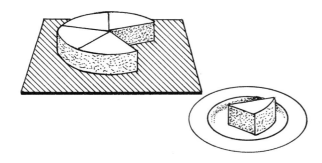

2 Barry takes a sixth of this cake.
What fraction does he leave for the others?

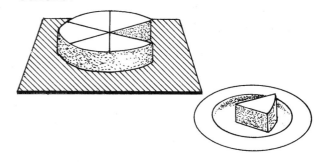

3 Look back at your shape cards.
For each shape say what fraction
is **not** coloured in.

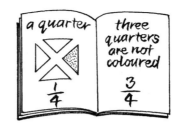

4 Three fifths $\left(\dfrac{3}{5}\right)$ of the curtain is patterned.

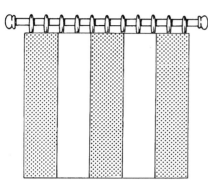

What fraction of the curtain is plain?

5 Four sevenths $\left(\dfrac{4}{7}\right)$ of the path is cracked.

What fraction of the path is not cracked?

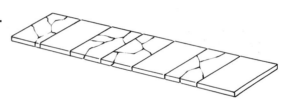

6

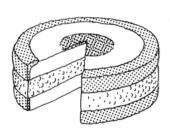

a One sixth $\left(\dfrac{1}{6}\right)$ of the pie is eaten.

What fraction of the pie is left?

b When $\dfrac{1}{3}$ is left, how much has been eaten?

7 The chocolate bar started with 8 pieces.

a What fraction has been eaten?

b What fraction is left?

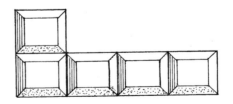

8 There are many ways of shading in half of a square.
Two are shown. How many more ways can you find?

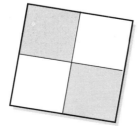

9 There are many ways of shading in three quarters of a square.
Two are shown.
Use a grid to help you find more ways.

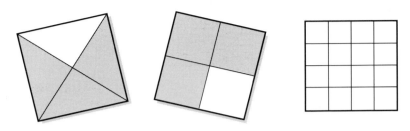

Ask your teacher for 'Fraction Rummy'.

A chessboard has 64 squares.

Half of the squares are black.

32 squares are black.

EXERCISE 4

1 There are four knights in a chess set.
Half of them are black.

Copy and complete: $\frac{1}{2}$ of 4 = ☐

2

A packet of sweets contains 10 chews.
Half of them are orange flavoured.

Copy and complete: $\frac{1}{2}$ of 10 = ☐

3 A stack is made from 6 draughts.
Half the stack is white.

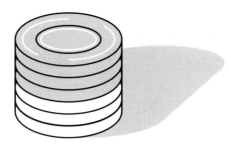

Copy and complete: $\frac{1}{2}$ of 6 = ▢

4 Copy and complete:

a $\frac{1}{2}$ of 8 = ▢   **b** $\frac{1}{2}$ of 16 = ▢   **c** $\frac{1}{2}$ of 20 = ▢

d $\frac{1}{2}$ of 30 = ▢   **e** $\frac{1}{2}$ of 24 = ▢   **f** $\frac{1}{2}$ of 50 = ▢

5

Minnie has a button collection.

a How many buttons are there?

b A quarter are square.
How many are square?

c Copy and complete: $\frac{1}{4}$ of 12 = ▢

6 Copy and complete:

a $\frac{1}{4}$ of 8 = ▢   **b** $\frac{1}{4}$ of 16 = ▢   **c** $\frac{1}{4}$ of 20 = ▢

d $\frac{1}{4}$ of 32 = ▢   **e** $\frac{1}{4}$ of 24 = ▢   **f** $\frac{1}{4}$ of 40 = ▢

7 The chocolate bar has 6 pieces.
A third of the bar is broken off.

a What is a third of 6?

b Copy and complete:

$\frac{1}{3}$ of 6 = ▢

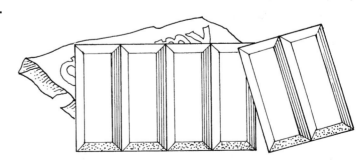

8 Copy and complete:

a $\frac{1}{3}$ of 9 = ▢   **b** $\frac{1}{3}$ of 15 = ▢   **c** $\frac{1}{3}$ of 21 = ▢

d $\frac{1}{3}$ of 30 = ▢   **e** $\frac{1}{3}$ of 27 = ▢   **f** $\frac{1}{3}$ of 60 = ▢

131

9 Copy and complete:

a $\frac{1}{5}$ of 10 = ⬜   **b** $\frac{1}{5}$ of 15 = ⬜   **c** $\frac{1}{5}$ of 20 = ⬜

d $\frac{1}{5}$ of 30 = ⬜   **e** $\frac{1}{5}$ of 25 = ⬜   **f** $\frac{1}{5}$ of 40 = ⬜

10 Copy and complete:

a $\frac{1}{6}$ of 12 = ⬜   **b** $\frac{1}{6}$ of 30 = ⬜   **c** $\frac{1}{6}$ of 42 = ⬜

d $\frac{1}{7}$ of 14 = ⬜   **e** $\frac{1}{7}$ of 21 = ⬜   **f** $\frac{1}{7}$ of 42 = ⬜

11 Copy and complete:

a $\frac{1}{8}$ of 8 = ⬜   **b** $\frac{1}{8}$ of 16 = ⬜   **c** $\frac{1}{8}$ of 24 = ⬜

d $\frac{1}{9}$ of 18 = ⬜   **e** $\frac{1}{9}$ of 27 = ⬜   **f** $\frac{1}{9}$ of 90 = ⬜

12

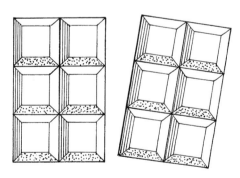 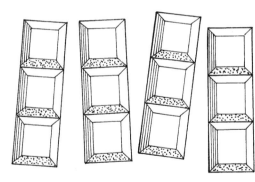

Jack breaks his bar into two halves.   Jill breaks her bar into four quarters.

He takes $\frac{1}{2}$.   She takes $\frac{2}{4}$.

a How many squares is half of a bar?

b How many squares is two quarters of a bar? $\boxed{\dfrac{1}{2} = \dfrac{2}{4}}$

13

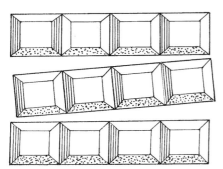

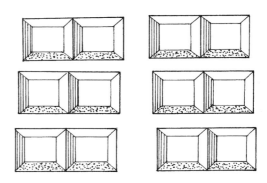

Mike breaks his bar into thirds.
He takes a third.

Nick breaks his bar into sixths.
He takes two sixths.

a How many squares is a third of a bar?

b How many squares is two sixths of a bar?

c Copy and complete: $\dfrac{1}{3} = \dfrac{\square}{6}$

14

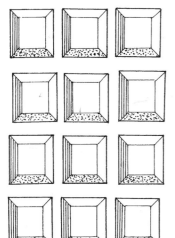

There are 12 squares in this bar.

a What fraction of the bar is one square?

b How many squares make half the bar?

c Copy and complete: $\dfrac{1}{2} = \dfrac{\square}{12}$

d How many squares make a third of the bar?

e Copy and complete: $\dfrac{1}{3} = \dfrac{\square}{12}$

f How many squares make a quarter of the bar?

g Copy and complete: $\dfrac{1}{4} = \dfrac{\square}{12}$

Do
Worksheet
2

CHECK-UP ON FRACTIONS

1

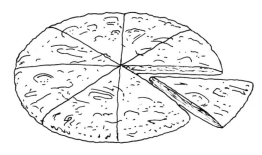

   a What fraction of the pizza is being removed?

   b What fraction of the pizza is left?

2 Two of the Cereal Selection packets are cornflakes.

   a What fraction of the selection is cornflakes?

   b What fraction of the selection is not cornflakes?

3 Copy and complete:

   a $\frac{1}{2}$ of 10 = ☐   **b** $\frac{1}{3}$ of 6 = ☐   **c** $\frac{1}{4}$ of 24 = ☐

   d $\frac{1}{5}$ of 30 = ☐   **e** $\frac{1}{6}$ of 6 = ☐   **f** $\frac{1}{7}$ of 35 = ☐

4

A quarter of the cards in Jim's hand are diamonds.

How many of the cards are diamonds?

5 $\frac{2}{6}$ of the hexagon has been shaded.

Name one other fraction which is the same as this.

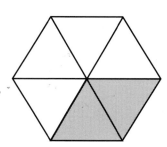

16 SOLVING MORE EQUATIONS

Guessing Games

Bryan and Jill are guessing numbers.

$4 \times$ $= 20$

Bryan works out that the hidden number is a 5, since

$4 \times 5 = 20$

EXERCISE 1

1 Work out these puzzles for Bryan.

a $+ 9 = 13$

b $15 -$ $= 10$

c $7 +$ $= 14$

d $- 2 = 19$

e $8 \times$ $= 16$

f $\times 2 = 12$

g $3 \times$ $= 21$

h $\times 4 = 20$

Jill writes some puzzles using the letter f for finger.

$2 \times$ $= 6$ becomes $2 \times f = 6$

2 Work out these puzzles for Bryan.

a $f + 3 = 10$

b $6 - f = 2$

c $8 + f = 12$

d $f - 1 = 9$

e $3 \times f = 15$

f $f \times 4 = 8$

Tidying Up

Every weekend Jill tidies up her room.
Here are some of the things she picks up.

3 books   4 tapes   5 pencils   2 coins

Making a quick note, she writes:

3*b* for 3 books   4*t* for 4 tapes   5*p* for 5 pencils   2*c* for 2 coins

EXERCISE 2

1 Use letters instead of words to tidy up the following.

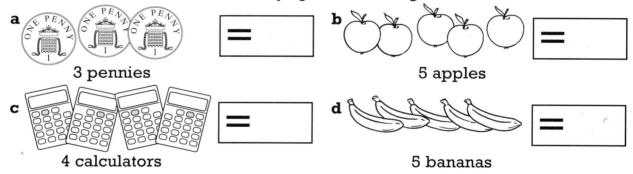

a 3 pennies   =   **b** 5 apples   =

c 4 calculators   =   **d** 5 bananas   =

2 This picture shows how
$4a + 2a = 6a$.

4 apples and 2 apples   =   6 apples

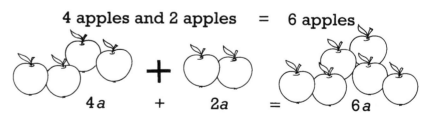

4*a*   +   2*a*   =   6*a*

What do these pictures show?

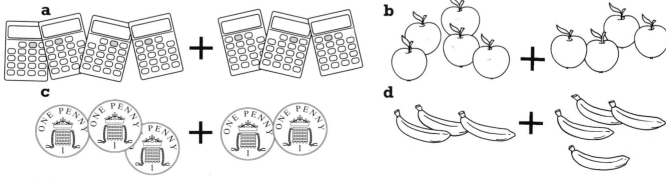

a

b

c

d

If we tidy up these, here is what we get:

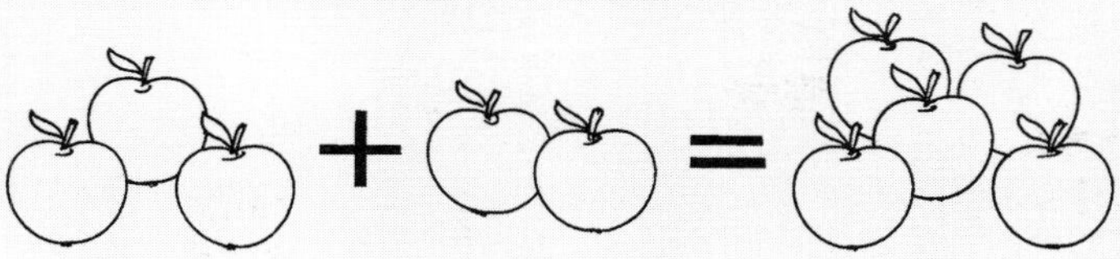

$3a + 2a = 5a$

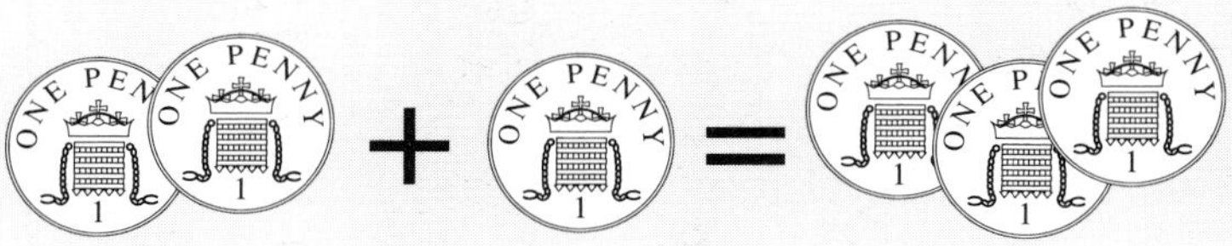

$2p + p = 3p$

EXERCISE 2B

1 Tidy up the following:

a

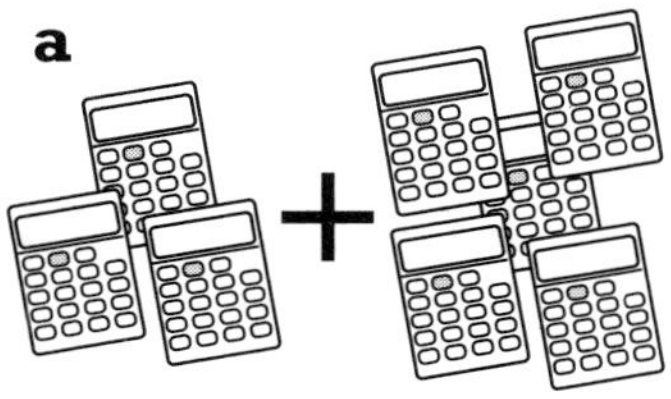

$3c + 5c =$

b

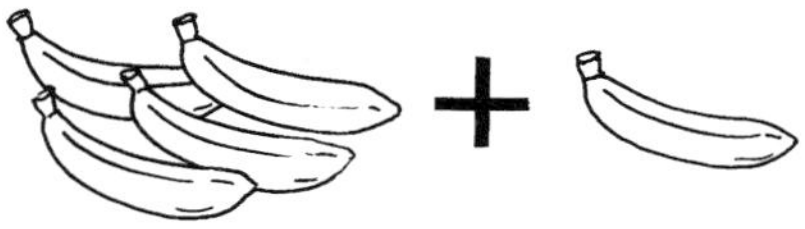

$4b + b =$

c

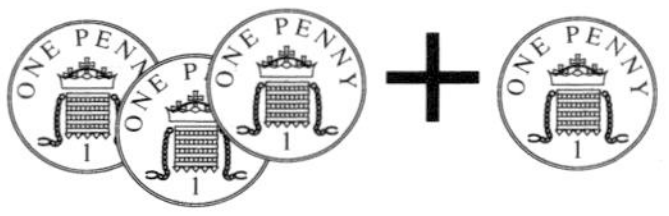

$3p + p =$

d

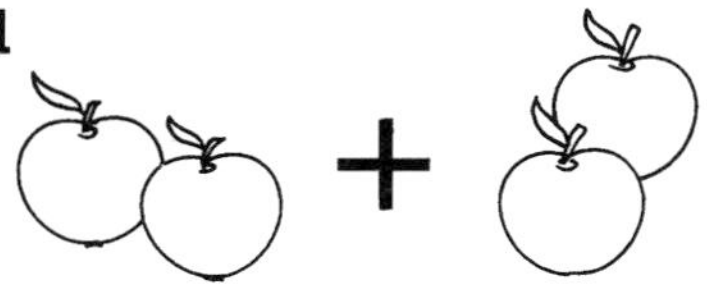

$2a + 2a =$

2 Now try these:

a $2a + 4a$ **b** $3b + 5b$ **c** $8c + 4c$

d $6x + 7x$ **e** $6y + y$ **f** $2x + x$

3 Look at this picture.

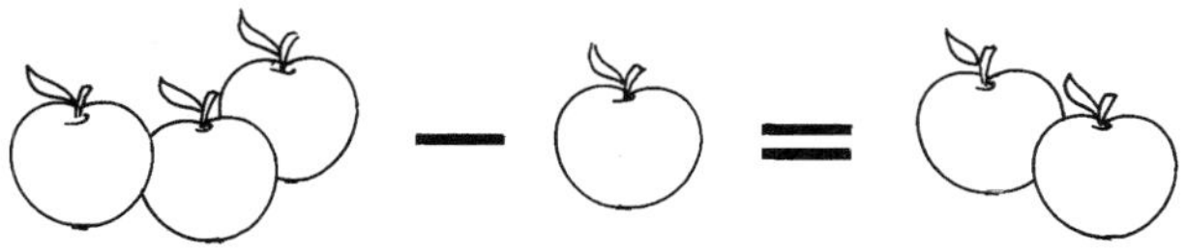

$3a - a = 2a$

Tidy up these in the same way:

a $7a - 2a$ **b** $8b - 4b$ **c** $4c - c$

d $x - x$ **e** $15y - 10y$ **f** $5x - 4x$

4 Now try these:

a $6a - a$ **b** $9b + 7b$ **c** $5c + 5c$

d $x + x$ **e** $10y - 9y$ **f** $7x - x$

How Many Marbles?

Martin puts the same number of
marbles in each jar.
We don't know how many!

We say there are *x* marbles in the jar when
we don't know how many there are.

This pictures shows *x* + 2 marbles.

EXERCISE 3

1 How many marbles are in each of the following pictures?

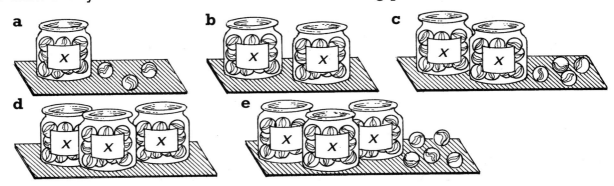

2 These jars have *y* marbles in each.
How many marbles are in each of these pictures?

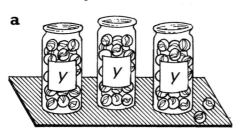

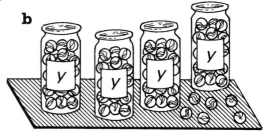

3 These jars are marked with the number of marbles inside.
How many marbles are in each picture?

Balancing scales

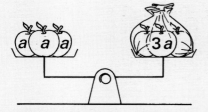

We know this scale balances ...

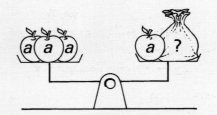

... so if this balances, then

? = 2a

EXERCISE 4

What is in each bag to make the scales balance?

1

2

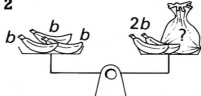

3

4 pppp

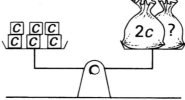

5

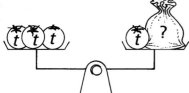

6

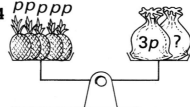

7

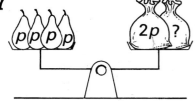

8

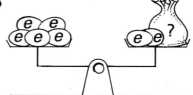

More Marbles

Two jars each with *a* marbles are emptied into a bigger jar.
There are 8 marbles altogether.
2*a* is the same as 8.

$$2a = 8 \qquad 2 \times a = 8$$

so $a = 4$

EXERCISE 5

1 What does each letter stand for in the following?

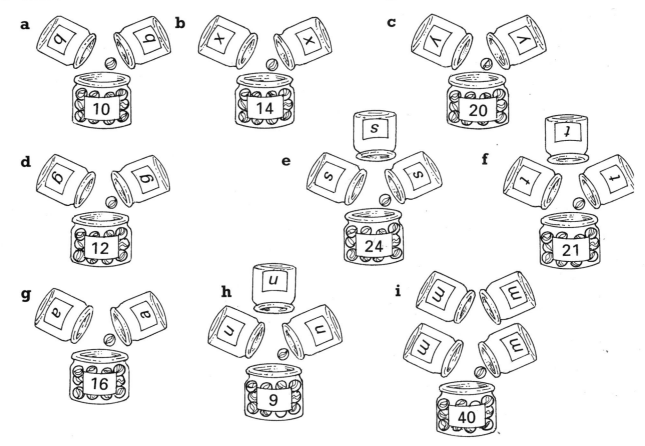

a 10

b 14

c 20

d 12

e 24

f 21

g 16

h 9

i 40

2 Now try these:

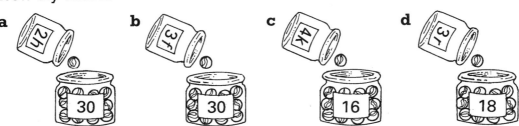

a 2h 30

b 3f 30

c 4k 16

d 3r 18

Mystery Weights

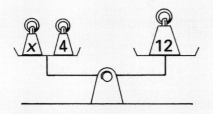

What must x be to make this balance?

$$x + 4 = 12$$
$$\text{so } x = 8$$
$$\text{since } 8 + 4 = 12$$

EXERCISE 5B

Find the mystery weight in each case.

1
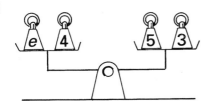

2

3
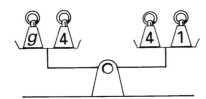

4

5
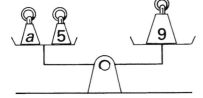

6
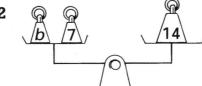

7

8
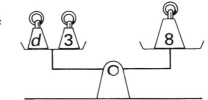

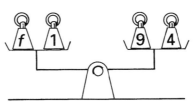

CHECK-UP ON MORE EQUATIONS

1 What number is the finger covering?

a  + 8 = 13

b 14 −  = 9

c $f \times 2 = 12$

d $7 - f = 6$

2 Use letters to tidy up the following:

a

2 bananas

b

4 eggs

c

1 apple

d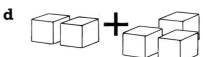

2 cubes and 3 cubes

3 Tidy up the following:
a $2x + 3x$ **b** $4y + 5y$ **c** $9x - x$

4 How many marbles are in each picture?

a

b

c

5 What is in the bag to
keep the scales balanced?

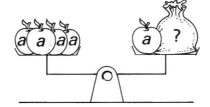

6 Find the mystery weight.

a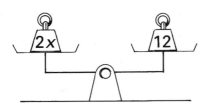

b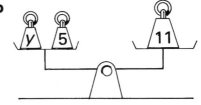

17 THREE DIMENSIONS

Properties

Some shapes roll, some pack, some slide and some stack.

Cube Cuboid Cylinder

Cone Sphere

EXERCISE 1

1 Here are some shapes in use.
 a What shape is being used?
 b What property is being used?

slide stack pack roll

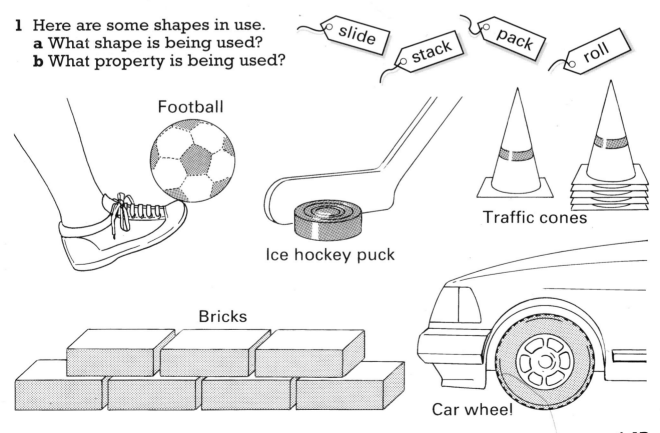

Football

Ice hockey puck

Traffic cones

Bricks

Car wheel

2 Name one property that both shapes have.
Use the labels.

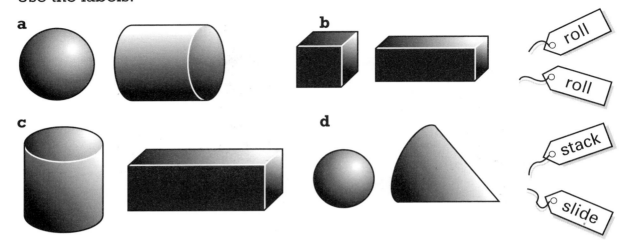

3 Name one thing that shape (i) can do that shape (ii) cannot.

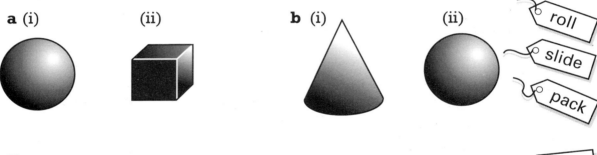

4 Here are some paper cups.
Match each label with picture
a, **b**, **c** or **d**.

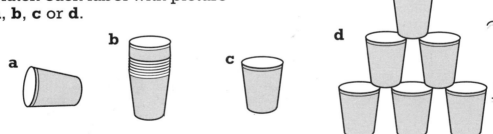

5 Some parts of a cylinder are **curved**. This lets it **roll**.

Some parts are **flat**. This lets it **slide**.

Some parts are **flat** and **parallel**. This lets it **stack**.

In a similar way, describe:
a the cone
b the cube.

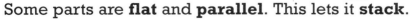

Features

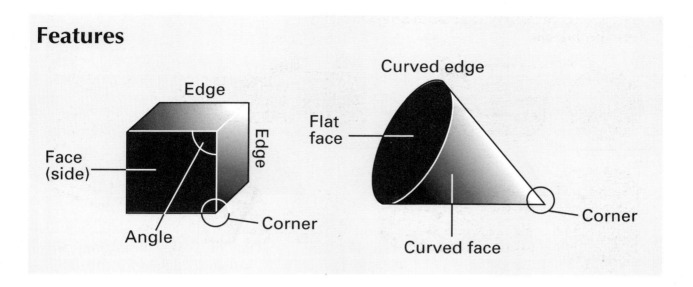

Edge

Edge

Face (side)

Angle

Corner

Curved edge

Flat face

Curved face

Corner

EXERCISE 2

1 A dice might help you to answer the following.

a How many faces does a cube have?
b How many edges does the cube have?
c Count the corners.
d How many right angles meet at each corner?
e What is the shape of each face?

2 A matchbox might help you to answer the following.

a How many faces does a cuboid have?
b How many edges does the cuboid have?
c Count the corners.
d How many right angles meet at each corner?
e What is the shape of each face?

3 A ball might help you to answer the following.

a How many faces does a sphere have?
b Does it have any edges?
c Does it have any corners?

Here are two more shapes.

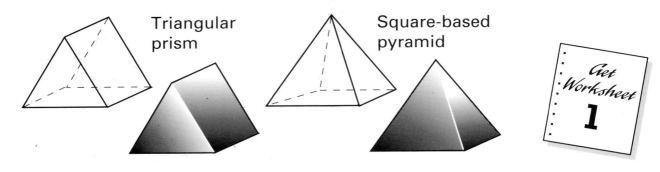

Triangular prism

Square-based pyramid

Get Worksheet
1

4 Copy and complete the table.

Name of solid	Number of faces	Number of edges	Number of corners
Cube	6	12	8
Cuboid			
Cylinder			
Sphere	1	0	0
Prism			
Pyramid			

5 A tent-maker wants to make a tent. He wants it to be a triangular prism. This includes a floor for the tent.

a How many rectangular pieces does he need?
b How many triangular pieces does he need?

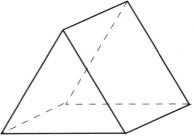

6 He also wants to make a small one-man tent. He wants it to be a square-based pyramid.

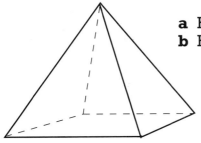

a How many squares will he need?
b How many triangles will he need?

7 A large tent is based on two simpler solids.
What are the names of the two solids?

Shapes formed from more than one simple solid are called **composite**.

EXERCISE 3

1 Jenny makes paper models by combining simpler shapes.
Name the simpler solids in each model below .

a

b

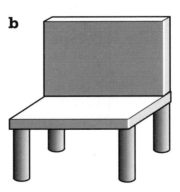

2 Frank makes a model town.
What solids does he use to make each building?

a

b

c

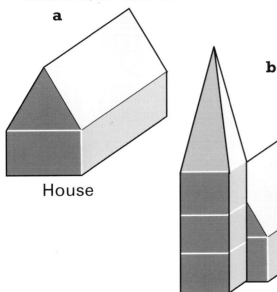

House

Church

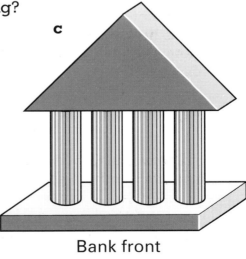

Bank front

CHECK-UP ON THREE DIMENSIONS

1 Name each solid.

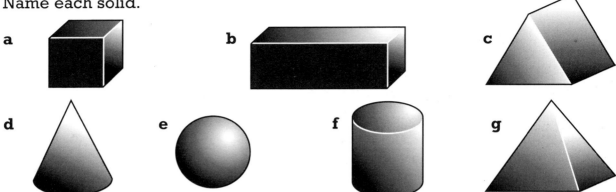

a   **b**   **c**

d   **e**   **f**   **g**

2 Which of the above solids:
  a slide   **b** stack   **c** roll?

3 What shapes are the faces of these solids?

 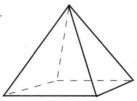 

  a cuboid   **b** pyramid   **c** the flat face of a cylinder

4 How many:
  (i) faces
  (ii) edges
  (iii) corners
are on ...

    a a cuboid   **b** a cylinder?

5

How many different solids can you spot in the model train? Name them.

18 PROBABILITY

What can it be?

Question

The referee spins the coin.

What results are possible?

Answer

Two results:

heads or tails

EXERCISE 1

1

Joey throws the dice.

Write down the numbers that are possible.

2 Meg spins this spinner.

Write down the two things that are possible.

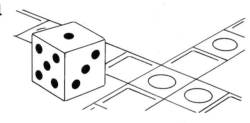

3 Jenny does a class survey.
She writes four flavours of crisps on a card.
She asks each pupil:
'Which of these flavours do you prefer?'

Name four possible flavours for her card.

4 Jack does a survey of car colours.
He makes a list for people to pick from.
Name four possible colours for his survey list.

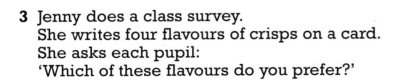

5 Jenny has nearly finished a game of Snakes and Ladders.

a What numbers on the dice will get her to the finish?

b What numbers on the dice will *not* get her to the finish?

6

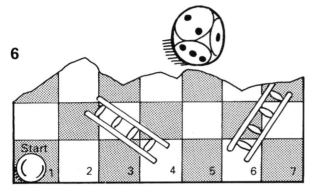

John is on square 1.

a What numbers on the dice will get him to the foot of a ladder?

b What numbers on the dice will not get him to the foot of a ladder?

Certain, possible or impossible?

It is Megan's turn to roll the dice.

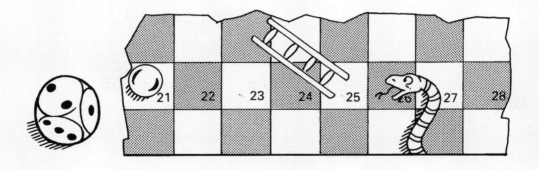

1 It is **certain** she will not stay on square 21.

2 It is **possible** that she will go up a ladder.

3 It is **possible** that she will go down a snake.

4 It is **impossible** for her to reach square 28.

EXERCISE 2

1 It is Samuel's turn.
Look at the board.
Say whether each statement is
certain, **possible** or **impossible**.
a He will not stay on square 66.
b He will go up a ladder.
c He will go down a snake.
d He will reach square 73.

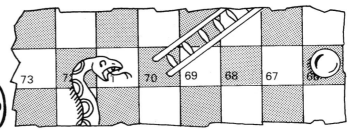

2 Which of the following is certain, possible or impossible
about the day after Monday?

   a The sun will rise.   **b** The sun will rise at noon.   **c** It will rain.

   d It will be Tuesday.   **e** You will be 5 years old again.   **f** It will be Thursday.

3

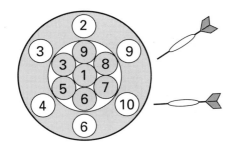

The match between Rovers and United was a draw.

Bryan and his friends tried to guess the actual
result. Here are their guesses:

2–1 0–0 1–3 2–2 0–1 4–1 1–1

a Which guesses cannot possibly be correct?
b Which guesses are possible?

4 Which of these totals are possible using only **two** of the five coins?

   a 4 pence
   b 11 pence
   c 6 pence
   d 20 pence
   e 16 pence

5

Two darts are thrown at this board.
Which of these scores are possible?
a A pair of fours
b A total of 16
c A dark 5 and a white 6
d A total of 20

6 Which label best fits each event?
   a If you score the most goals, you win.
   b Wednesday comes after Tuesday.
   c Easter Sunday is Tuesday 17 April.
   d It will snow in January.
   e 2 + 2 = 5
   f Spin a coin and get tails.
   g If you score no goals, you lose.

Certain   Possible   Impossible

More or Equally Likely?

Some events are **more likely** than others.
1 It is more likely to snow in winter than in summer.
2 Throw a dice and there is a better chance of getting a number less than 5 than a number greater than 5.

Some events are **equally likely**.
1 The chances are even that you remove your right shoe before your left shoe.
2 When you open a book you have an even chance of picking an odd numbered page.

EXERCISE 3

1 Choose the more likely event from each pair.

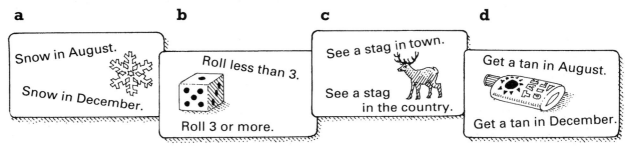

    a   **b**   **c**   **d**

- a Snow in August. / Snow in December.
- b Roll less than 3. / Roll 3 or more.
- c See a stag in town. / See a stag in the country.
- d Get a tan in August. / Get a tan in December.

2 What can be said about these two pairs?

Pick a black card / Pick a red card

Come up heads / Come up tails

3 Which label best fits each of these events?
  a Reading the time from a sundial at midnight.
  b Picking the ace of spades from a pack.
  c Getting an even number when you roll a dice.
  d You will win the lottery.
  e Tomorrow will be dry.
  f A Christmas menu will have turkey.
  g A domino will have at least one dot on it.
  h A piece of toast falls and lands butter-side up.
  i A watched kettle never boils.
  j Christmas will come in December.

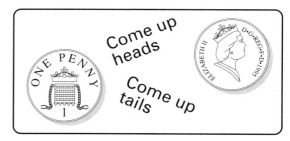

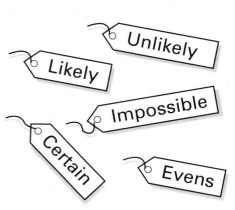

Unlikely
Likely
Impossible
Certain
Evens

4 Look at this line. It shows how likely five particular events are.

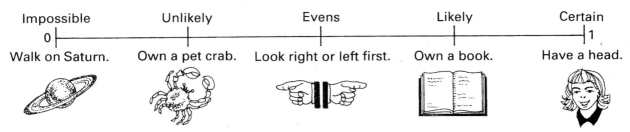

Impossible	Unlikely	Evens	Likely	Certain
Walk on Saturn.	Own a pet crab.	Look right or left first.	Own a book.	Have a head.

Make up your own 'Likelihood Line'.

Fairness

A game is fair when everyone has the same chance of winning.

You can win 2 ways.
The wheel operator can win 6 ways.
The wheel is *not* fair.

You can win 4 ways.
The wheel operator can win 4 ways.
The wheel is fair.

EXERCISE 4

1 Alan and Azra play with this spinner.
Alan wins when it lands on a circle.
Azra wins if it lands on a blank.

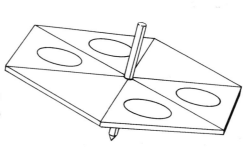

a How many circles are on the spinner?
b How many blanks are on the spinner?
c Is the spinner fair?

2 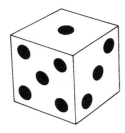 Lisa and Tim cast the dice.
Tim says: 'I win if the number is bigger than 3.
You win if it is less than 3.'

a How many numbers let Tim win?
b How many numbers let Lisa win?
c Are the rules fair?

3 Tom, Pat and Jan are playing with this spinner. It is *not* a fair spinner.

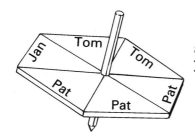

a Who gets the best deal from the spinner?
b What would you change to make the spinner fair?

4 Adam, Bill and Charlie play a game.
They throw two coins in the air.
Adam wins if two heads appear.
Bill wins if two tails appear.
Charlie wins if there is one head and one tail.

Look at the pictures of how a 5p and a 1p might fall.

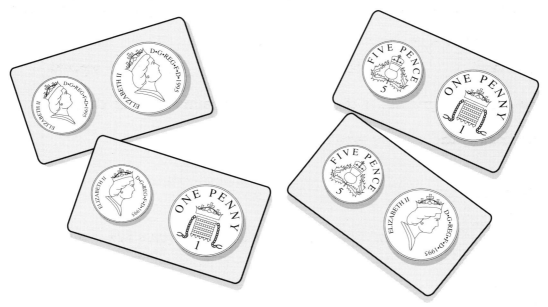

a How many ways can Adam win?
b How many ways can Bill win?
c How many ways can Charlie win?
d Is this fair?

CHECK-UP ON PROBABILITY

1 Choose the best label to describe each event.

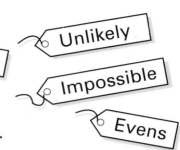

a It will snow on Christmas day.
b A dice will come up a 4.
c $3 \times 3 = 9$.
d A coin will land heads.
e A playing card picked from the pack will be over 4.

2 Sita is on square 14 and it is her shot.

a Which type of square is she most likely to land on?

(i) a snake's head   (ii) a ladder   (iii) an empty square

b Which square in the picture is it impossible to reach with one throw?

c Which squares in the picture will she certainly not be on?

3 Which of these are fair?

a   Spinning a coin to see who goes first.

b    An odd number means I start.
An even number means you start.

c 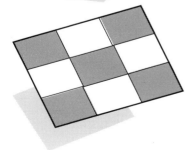   John and Claudia throw coins at this board.
If a coin lands on a black square, John wins.
If a coin lands on a white square, Claudia wins.
If a coin lands on a line, they throw again.